Pilot or Passenger

PILOT

OR

PASSENGER

7 Raw Facts to take control and
create the life you desire

ALEX BONETT

Printed and bound in Australia by BookPOD

Disclaimer
The material in this book is general comment only and neither purports nor intends to be specific advice related to any particular reader. It does not represent professional advice and should not be relied on as the basis for any decision or action on any matter that it covers. To the maximum extent permitted by law, the author and publisher disclaim all responsibility and liability to any person or entity, whether a purchaser or not, in respect to anything and of the consequences of anything done by any such person in reliance, whether in whole or in part, upon the whole or any part of the contents of this publication.

A Catalogue-in-Publication is available from the National Library of Australia.

ISBN: 978-0-9944812-0-7

Acknowledgements

Wow! My book is finally a reality.

They say that where we are at any given moment is the culmination of a lifetime of experiences, interactions, choices and actions.

So to is this book, it's essentially a short collection from my 'Highlights and Lowlight Mental Movie Reel' of my life so far. I have written it to share some of my main life changing experiences and most importantly the lessons and learning's from the amazing opportunities and experiences thus far.

Traditionally book acknowledgements, are a dedication to all the "Wonderful People" that have influenced the author...Well as this book is based on "Raw Facts" I would also like to thank those people who in one form or another have brought grief, misery and heartache into my world. To you, and you know who you are, I now say thank you for the experience and wisdom you have given me and helping me become the person I am today.

As for the Amazing and Wonderful people in my life, thank you form the bottom of my heart. You have all given me so much joy, laughter, love and support. I am eternally grateful.

In particular my father, who was an illiterate post war migrant, you instilled in me your amazing work ethic and you always had a smile for everyone.

Bob Baily. Bob, what can I say? Mentor, father figure and role model – when I grow up I want to be like you! Thank you for your belief in me and your continual support, your hard love and for teaching me to question my own thinking and to look at the World through the eyes of a five year old.

To 'The Eagles', Andrew Wise, Gary Tuck, Stephen Hogg, for your support and collectively creating one of the most amazing corporate management teams possible. What a wonderful, once in a lifetime chapter that I will always cherish.

To my ex-wife Cheryle, thank you for a wonderful twenty years of love, & support and continued friendship.

To Edith, for you professional help, understand and encouragement. You helped me claw my way up from my abyss. I am eternally grateful and I promise to help others as you have helped me.

My dearest friends, Steve & Renee, and Lorraine. And all For just being there with unquestioning love and support.

To Helen MacDonald and Scott Stein, thank you for the many opportunities, your belief in me and your inspiration.

My clients and the hundreds of people that have taken the time to write or call with your feedback, testimonials and success stories of how I have played some part in the positive changes in their lives – I am truly humbled and grateful.

Tim Vanderlay, my Transcriber and writing mentor, for your great energy, inspiration, guidance and patience. Lauren Shay my proofreader and Sylvie for the design, and publishing – Thank you all so much for helping me make this book a reality.

And to two very special people: Aida and her amazing son Angus. Thank you so much for your love, belief and inspiration and encouragement. You have given me more special moments in the past few years than in the entire fifty-three before we met. Thank you so very much.

In closing I would like to say that I am so grateful of everything in my life even the hard bits.

CONTENTS

REFLECT

ACHIEVE

THINK

LIFE

ACT

LEARN

PLAN

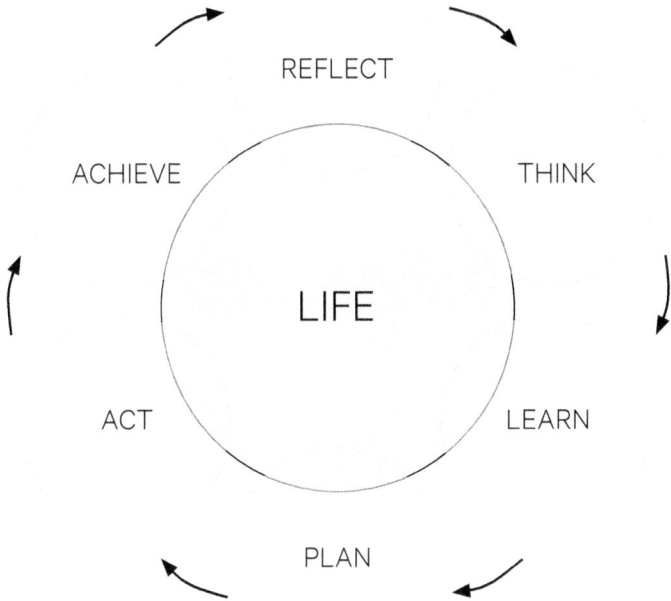

EMBRACE AND LEARN FROM LIFE'S CHALLENGES
TO CREATE A BETTER TOMORROW.

I have a story I believe is worth sharing. However, my story is not complete. It has a beginning, a middle and a desired end, but fortunately that end hasn't come to pass. Despite this, I want to share my story with you because while my highs have been great, my lows have taken me to depths I never thought I would go to. I have also learnt that most of us will experience similar highs and lows at one time or another during our journeys here on Earth, so we have something in common.

What we have most in common is that we are all on a journey with an infinite number of possible destination... sometimes the ride gets choppy and we feel out of control.

What we have most in common is that we are all on a journey with an infinite number of possible destinations. A journey that can reveal to us an incomprehensible number of paths, stopovers, and mind-expanding wonders. Unfortunately, it's not always a smooth and uneventful journey—an easy flight with favourable winds and bright sunshine. Sometimes the ride gets choppy and we feel out of control.

Today, I ask you to stop and ask yourself this question:

On your life's flight path, are you the Pilot or the Passenger?

You know that when you're a Passenger, you have no control over where the plane is going. When there's turbulence, all you can do is hang on and hope things turn out well. Many people go through life as Passengers, safely sitting at the back of the plane with all the other Passengers, their fate and destination in the hands of others, hoping and trusting that the pilot is competent and remains on course. Delays, takeoffs, speed, altitude, negotiating storms and turbulence, dealing with emergencies—they are all up to someone else. Even the food you are served and the views you take in are determined by others.

This can be comfortable, of course, and there's safety in numbers. But the reality is that the people who settle for being Passengers abdicate their responsibility for their life's journey. If something goes wrong, they blame someone else. Sure, they get to their destination with little trouble, but they can't change course.

That's what I call a "discount package" life. It comes with no frills and it's comfortable, but in the end, it's unsatisfying. I want to share my unfinished story with you to show you there's another way; another choice that will help you take your place in the pilot's seat and take command of your journey.

If up to this point you've been a Passenger in your life, today is the day you take back the controls, reset your flight plan, do your checks and cross checks, and take off toward the life you know you should be living and deserve. That's what this book is about. You're reading it because you know you can do better. You can be more. You can have more wealth, more satisfaction and more achievement. You have a gap, an unsatisfied yearning for a better life. You have dreams, a vision of a wonderful and fulfilling journey. Today, take the controls. If you're serious, then learn from my story. Don't say: "This doesn't apply to me." That's just an excuse for inaction. Instead, ask yourself: "How can I use this to change the course of my life?"

Today is your day! Grab it with both hands. You're clear for takeoff!

Your Flight Path

In this book, I'm going to share with you the Seven Raw Facts that I've learnt, through real-life experience, so you can take control and set your flight path for real change. What is a flight path? The details differ for every person, but every flight path covers these six stages:

Reflect—Think—Learn—Plan—Act—Achieve

So far, my flight path has been from school flunky and trolley boy to corporate executive, business creator, author, speaker and mentor.

So far, my flight path has been from school flunky and trolley boy to corporate executive, business creator, author, speaker and mentor.

It's been an amazing journey; rough at times, humbling at others, but never uneventful.

Because my journey has been so interesting, I've been thinking about this book for a long time, but it's been taking shape for even longer. When I was at school, I faced the challenge of being partially dyslexic and somewhat "scholastically challenged". Back then, of course, teachers didn't pay attention to that sort of thing; they just thought you were being disruptive or difficult. But when I was 15 years old, everything changed: I got my first part-time job with supermarket chain Safeway (back then it was called "Red S"), packing customers' groceries.

On Thursday nights and Saturday mornings, I would put on my stylish red vest (with a matching red bow tie, certain to attract attention from young ladies) and spend my shift packing groceries in old-fashioned brown paper bags. We were called Red Coats and there were 14 of us in all, including the Head Red Coat. The Head Red Coat would look after the front of the store and do price checks, while one of us would be on trolley collection and the rest of us would pack customers' orders. The supermarket had 12 checkouts, so before our shift the Head Red Coat would put 12 pieces of paper, numbered 1 to 12, in a hat and each of us would draw a number. The number we drew was the number of the checkout we would pack behind. All we hoped for was to be able to pack behind a cute "check-out chick".

At school, I rarely received compliments or praise, but I soon discovered that if I was friendly and nice to customers, and packed their groceries really well, they would thank me with a big smile and sometimes even give me a tip. Early in my career, one lady gave me a 50 cent tip! That doesn't sound like much now, but keep in mind that at the time I was earning 67 cents per hour. The compliments, tips and attention from customers and my manager made me feel great.

At school, I rarely received compliments or praise, but I soon discovered that if I was friendly and nice to customers, and packed their groceries really well, they would thank you with a big smile and sometimes even give you a tip.

My attitude was that I was there to please and do as I was told: Yes Sir, No Sir, three bags full Sir. I felt a sense of purpose and belonging, and I loved it. I thrived in this environment and the more attention and positive feedback I received, the harder and faster I worked. It wasn't too long before I got a big break: the Head Red Coat left and I was promoted to his position! Imagine: me, Head Red Coat, at the tender age of 15 years. In my mind, I was going to be the best Head Red Coat ever.

I had found my niche, something I was good at no matter what most of my teachers thought of me. Despite my reading and learning problems, I finally finished high school with a score of 67/300 for my efforts. Fortunately, with 2 years of causal experience, a good reputation and a small white lie regarding my school results... Safeway offered me a cadetship. This was a new program from the United States. I was one of 22 fresh-faced, eager young employees selected from across the state to participate in a three-year training program designed to teach us all about the supermarket industry, from the ground up.

The program brought out my competitive side and I thrived. I went on to become one of Safeway's youngest store managers, and had a terrific 10-year career with the company. By the time I was 25, full of confidence and my own self-importance, there was nothing about retail I didn't know ... or so I thought. You can't tell a 25-year-old anything, right? By this point, I had transferred to Queensland and had managed three stores at three different shopping centres. Each of these shopping centres had a family-owned fruit market that was a direct competitor to Safeway, and the matriarch of the family business was always saying: "Alex, why are you working so hard for them? You should come and join us. You should open your own business with us."

Finally, the siren song of a new challenge got the best of me and I jumped ship. With all my knowledge and experience, what could go wrong?

Hero to Zero

Talk about going from hero to zero in the blink of an eye! If you have ever been in a partnership, you probably know what I'm talking about. I had been with one company for 10 years since high school and, in many ways, had been sheltered from the real world. I had a heart as white as snow, was trusting and naïve, and thought I was much smarter than I was.

My new business partners turned out to be well known to law-enforcement authorities ... they saw me and my money as easy pickings — and they were right.

My new business partners turned out to be well known to law-enforcement authorities and were, in fact, suspected of being associated with a particularly active terrorist organisation. They saw me and my money as easy pickings — and they were right. I invested all my money in this family-owned chain, but I neglected to get anything in writing. They kept saying, "Alex, don't worry, we'll write it up later." The only good thing about this episode of my life was that they financially plundered me quickly — they didn't drag it on for months. They lured me into their den and spat out my bones — and with these people, there was definitely no complaints department!

They took everything I had: I lost my house and all my possessions, and found myself living in a friend's garage with six boxes of belongings and my leased car out in front — because everybody knows that when you have a business, you have to lease a great car you can't afford, right? I had been an overly confident, overly trusting, naïve fool and paid the price.

My saving grace was that I had lots of contacts in the supermarket and fresh-food industry. I knew a guy whose family owned the premier fresh food retail outlet in Queensland, and we had a talk. He wanted to expand; he had the money, but not the people he could trust. On the other hand, I had no money but I had sweat equity, a lot of knowledge and an overwhelming desire not to starve. He offered me a role in his business that would let me bring all my knowledge to the table. I teamed with him and his son and, in a few years, we built the second-largest chain of fresh-food markets in Australia.

Five great years later, the business sold and I went for my first real job interview with the Australian petroleum company, Ampol. Buoyed by my achievements, I was back to being brash, overconfident and full of self-importance. But the people at Ampol must have seen something, because they hired me as a Franchise Business Adviser. Ampol had formed a joint venture with another company – Finemore's Transport, one of Australia's leading transport and logistics companies. The joint-venture company was called Ampol Road Pantry, and my role was to assist it in setting up a new national network of franchised convenience stores. That's where I met the general manager, a wonderful gentleman named Bob Bailey, who became my mentor and had a profound influence on my life. More on Bob later.

Things continued to move fast. My work was exciting and rewarding on many levels — the team of people I was involved with were and still are amazing. Over time, I was promoted to general manager. Then, after nine amazing years, the company was sold to Caltex. I was given the opportunity to join the Caltex team, but instead I accepted an offer to join Finemore Transport as its general manager of warehousing and logistics. I'd had no previous experience in this field, but figured a 30-year shortcut to the top was too great an opportunity to pass.

... I clawed my way over mountains of resistance, mostly from my own senior management team, some of whom were very keen to see this new kid on the block fail.

My job was to effect, more or less, a complete turnaround of Finemore's internal culture. I was to convince the 1,250 employees in my division that they weren't just truck drivers and warehouse personnel, but were in Customer Service! It was an uphill battle and, believe me, it took every bit of my will and determination. For the next two years, I clawed my way over mountains of resistance, mostly from my own senior management team, some of whom were very keen to see this new kid on the block fail. Over time, I had some successes, particularly with some of our most disgruntled customers – all of whom supported my endeavours. I was on a great salary with great benefits, but I was working 25 hours a day, eight days a week, and I started to realise that I didn't have a life.

Cemeteries Are Full of Irreplaceable People

Around this time, I received some very sad news: the wife of a great friend of mine from the old Ampol team, Andrew, had died of cancer. She was only 32 and they had two young children. There was no way I was not going to attend her funeral to pay my respects and support my friend. But over the next few days, I could hardly believe how hard it was to reschedule my meetings and appointments so I could attend.

Finally, I managed to juggle my schedule and make it. While I was there, I had a sobering moment of clarity. Firstly, I thought: "This really sucks. She was 32 years old and she's dead, and these two kids are going to grow up without their mother." This made me feel numb and sad. Hard on the heels of that, I thought: "It should never be this hard to get away from work to attend a friend's funeral." This made me feel not numb, but dumb! What was I doing?

In the following few months, I couldn't get those thoughts out of my mind. On the surface, I was successful, but at what cost? What kind of life was I living? Then the universe decided to really drive the point home: my state manager was seeking to fill a position for a senior contract manager. During the selection process, I met the finalist – a 52-year-old guy named Kevin. He was an absolute gentleman with loads of experience and enthusiasm. He was selected for the position and he was over the moon about the opportunity to work with us. A few weeks after starting, he stopped by my office to chat, all the while stretching and saying that his back was playing up. As someone who has suffered with chronic back pain, I empathised with him and suggested he talk to the office manager about getting a different office chair.

A few months later, that lower back pain turned out to be spinal cancer. This man, who was full of ideas and excitement — ready to give it all for his new role —was struck down. He kept working for

9

as long as he could but sadly passed away just a few months later. I couldn't believe it.

After Kevin could no longer work, I would walk by his vacant office. Where a few weeks ago had sat a vibrant, enthusiastic, model employee, there was an empty chair and bare desk, lights out, computer off. The corporate wheel stops for no one, and the recruitment process to fill Kevin's position had already begun. A few weeks later, there was a new person behind that desk; a fresh face full of enthusiasm, hope and dreams.

I flashed on something that Bob Bailey, my mentor, had said to me years earlier, a statement with profound meaning that I finally understood in full. "Alex," he said, "It doesn't matter how important you think you are ... cemeteries are full of irreplaceable people."

This got me really thinking about my life. I found myself sitting through management meetings, jotting down destination points for future fishing trips. I love fishing and one of my dreams had always been to go camping and fishing all around Australia. I couldn't escape the idea that I was missing out on something amazing. I couldn't help thinking that Andrew's wife and Kevin had both thought they had plenty of time to follow their dreams. After some serious thinking, I decided to do the scariest thing I had ever done and hand in my resignation.

Tossing in a senior position with a six-figure salary and benefits, with no alternate employment and a mortgage, is not the easiest (or wisest) thing to do, but in hindsight it was one of my best decisions ever!

Tossing in a senior position with a six-figure salary and benefits, with no alternate employment and a mortgage, is not the easiest (or wisest) thing to do, but in hindsight it was one of my best decisions ever! The managing director couldn't believe I was resigning to go fishing. He thought it was crazy; nobody does that. He was sure I had been lured away by a competitor. "Who are you going to work for?" he asked me over and over. Finally, I got him to understand that I was, in fact, just going fishing. He still thought I was crazy but asked if I could stay for a while to tie up a few loose ends.

At that time, a family-owned boating and fishing retailer was looking for a general manager, and I thought: "The holiday can wait – this would be a great job where I could marry my hobby and passion with my work!" So I took the job. Another dumb decision. I still remember Bob asking me in his typical thought-provoking style, "AB, are you sure you want to go and work for a family-owned business, reporting to two brothers and their wives?"

Bob was a wise man. After just three months into the role, we parted company. I had learnt another valuable lesson: never allow emotions to overrule logic. I'd learnt how easily we can kid ourselves into seeing what we want to see and ignore the obvious signs of danger. The business owners and I parted company and I was back on track for my dream holiday!

A month later, I took delivery of my second-hand four-wheel drive and my new boat, and in January 2000 my partner Cheryle and I rented out our home and headed off for the adventure of a lifetime.

On the Wallaby

That was the beginning of a glorious 10 months. We drove around Australia, lived in a tent and fished. Amazingly, I spent the first month looking for things to worry about. After all, I was a problem solver, and my corporate instincts were still active; I just didn't know how to relax. But over time, I got the hang of letting go and it was great. It was time of clarity and perspective for me, and when I finally returned to the real world, I had changed. I had a new perspective on life. Things I had thought were critically important before the trip weren't so important any more, and things that hadn't been important previously had become very important.

While on the road—or, as it's referred to in Australia, "on the Wallaby", hopping from one place to the next — we met many interesting and wonderful people of all ages and backgrounds. Some were long-term travellers who had been on the road for two, three, five years or more, while others were just getting away for a month or two and dreaming of their "Big Trip". But the one common thread was that we were all looking for that balance; that ability to take in deep breaths of fresh air, shake off the shackles of contemporary life and break out of "the Matrix", if only for a little while. We were all living the dream.

The lure of money, position and ego is tempting, and it was hard on more than one occasion to say: "Thanks, but no thanks."

While I was on my journey, a couple of headhunters contacted me, offering me some wonderful opportunities in various executive roles. But I knew that if I accepted, my dream trip would come to an untimely end and I would fall straight back into the life I had walked away from. The lure of money, position and ego is tempting, and it was hard on more than one occasion to say: "Thanks, but no thanks." But I did. I promised one particularly persistent (but nice) headhunter that I would call him within a few days of my return to Melbourne.

After 10 months, we were camping on a beach in the southeast corner of Australia and it was starting to get cold. I even had to use my windscreen wipers for the first time in months. It was time to head home, which was still 3,500 kilometres away, and included crossing the magnificent Nullarbor Plain and skirting the Great Australian Bight. A month later, we arrived home but I returned with a new and humble appreciation for life and the world around me.

Wake-Up Call

Five days after I returned home, I honoured my promise and called the headhunter. He was delighted to hear I was back and started rattling off a few positions he felt I was guaranteed to get. We arranged to meet at his office the following week. For the next few days, I wandered around my house almost tripping on my bottom lip; I had a bad case of "the sads". Eventually, I rang the headhunter back and cancelled the appointment. I didn't know exactly what I wanted to do, but I knew exactly what I didn't want to do: get sucked back into the Matrix.

I felt I had a story to tell, and some valuable insights and lessons to share. This was the start of a new and exciting path for me: I wanted to create a living where I had flexibility, where I could help others succeed, and where I could find balance and grow. I truly appreciated that life is a journey we should enjoy. If you focus on the wrong areas and plan to enjoy life later, later may never come. I had heard this in various forms many times over the years, but I was now a true believer – and the message really hit home.

If you focus on the wrong areas and plan to enjoy life later, later may never come.

About a year after I returned from our odyssey, Cheryle and I headed to Brisbane for a friend's wedding. We allowed a month to explore, camp and relax along the 1,800 kilometres of coastline between Melbourne and Brisbane. The night after the wedding I stayed at my best friend Macca's house, intending to drive about five hours to the Tamworth Country Music Festival the next day. But I woke at 3am with a fever and chills, and by 6am I could barely move my ankles. Every joint was aching: it felt like I had been beaten with a baseball bat.

I was a little concerned. Over the past few weeks, I had camped in a few places that were infested with mosquitoes, and Dengue Fever and Ross River Fever were very much on my mind. I thought to myself, "Well, you got it this time!" Over the next few hours, the aches, pains and fever got worse.

At 8am, Cheryle took me to the local doctor. I shuffled in like Frankenstein's monster and spent 30 minutes with a lovely old physician who was genuinely concerned about my condition, but unsure of what it was. He took some blood tests, told me to come back in the morning for the results and sent me home. Within a few hours, I couldn't stand the light and couldn't even swallow water.

The last thing I remember was sitting on the edge of the bed, foraging in my suitcase for something. Cheryle came into the room and asked what I was looking for and I remember shouting back, "I don't know!" I recall her saying, "I'm calling an ambulance to take you to hospital," to which I vaguely recall saying: "No, I'm seeing the doctor in the morning." The next thing I remember was waking in the intensive care unit of the Mater Hospital in Brisbane. I'd been in a coma for three days.

The next thing I remember was waking in the intensive care unit of the Mater Hospital in Brisbane. I'd been in a coma for three days.

I had contracted Meningococcal Meningitis. The doctors estimated that had I been home alone, I would have slipped into unconsciousness and died within six hours. As it was, I was only a few hours away from having both my feet amputated.

After my recovery, I reflected on this event. I had lived, relatively unscathed, through a remarkable life lesson: *life is about choices*. I could wait for circumstances to force change upon me, or I could choose to change things. This episode raised my bar yet again.

Change or Be Changed

With that uncompromising perspective to guide me, I started doing some business consulting. I bought a license to sell marketing programs for businesses and started introducing myself to business owners by inviting them to free two-hour seminars. My obsessions with customer service, grass-roots marketing and helping people to live the lifestyles they wanted helped me connect with my audiences. People were interested in my story and my journey thus far, and how they could take the next step.

Through my consulting and mentoring practice, I learnt quickly that there are a lot of people out there who only get motivated when the bank manager is knocking at their door. I found myself caring more about some people's businesses than they did. I was not only teaching but learning a great deal from my interactions with my clients and audiences. I got a clear picture of people's motivation for getting into business, their inability or unwillingness to use their business to make their lives better, and their blame mentality when things go wrong. In turn, I found myself searching, studying, observing and learning about the psychology behind success and failure.

With those insights and my passion to share, teach and inspire, I was able to gain the trust of numerous companies and spent the next 12 years delivering keynote presentations and training programs on the psychology of sales and the art of delivering "Awesome Customer Service". Even people who didn't see themselves as salespeople soon realised that everyone sells *something* for a living, even if they're just selling themselves. We're all in the persuasion business. But most people have little understanding of the psychology behind sales, service and success.

The purpose of this book is to distill 40 years of practical, grass-roots, warts-and-all experiences into real-world advice that I call the Raw Facts. It's the knowledge, drive and motivation that took me from trolley boy to senior executive to entrepreneur. I want to share with you the central piece of wisdom I've learned:

> *The purpose of this book is to distill 40 years of practical, grass-roots, warts-and-all experiences into real-world advice that I call the 'Raw Facts'.*

If you understand, accept and embrace some basic truths, and follow some simple principles without complicating things too much, you can enjoy the career and life you've always wanted.

The heart of my approach is simple: most of us attach the greatest importance to the wrong parts of our lives and careers. We keep our noses to the grindstone and think that's going to bring us what we want, but we often end up with skinned noses and empty lives. I see people fixated on consumerism, rating their success by the things they accumulate: "want, want, want, gimme gimme, gimme." Some people fall under the spell of money without realising that while money is good and having it is better than not having it, money is not everything. We treat the enjoyment of life as an impediment to making money when the opposite is true: money is a tool to help us get the greatest joy out of life. Don't let life get in the way of living.

If you create the lifestyle you want, take time to smell the roses, go for a walk and really savour life, you'll be better, sharper and filled with more energy for whatever you do, which will make you more successful at it. But even if it didn't, the Raw Facts would still be worth listening to. In 100 years, we'll all be dead. There are millions of people every morning who head off to work to their little cells where they do mindless work. Their biggest objective is making it to Friday night. Sadly, studies show that 60 per cent of people are disengaged with their work. Another 30 per cent of people are dissatisfied and unhappy with their personal relationships. That's a lot of unhappy people.

Sound familiar? If you're not careful, you may find yourself being a passenger through life arriving safely to death! You can easily get sucked into the Matrix. You might buy things to assuage your unhappiness and to anaesthetise yourself. You start out as a "gonna", as in, "I'm gonna do that one day." Then as you get older, you become a "shoulda", as in, "I shoulda done that when I was still young enough." Then one day, you die. You're a cautionary tale.

Nobody wants "They was a cautionary tale" on their gravestone. If that's you, what I have to share may be your wake up call.

Of course, you would be justified in asking, "Alex, why should we listen to you?" Why, because of my boyish charm! All right, maybe that's not reason enough. So what about this: I was told many years ago, "You have to go through a lot of rubble in order to find the gems." Well, I've shovelled tonnes of rubble during my journey and done a lot of the hard yards and have kept the rubble out of this book. I've made sure that you don't have to dig too hard to find the gems; I've done the digging for you.

I was told many years ago, "You have to go through a lot of rubble in order to find the gems."

But the other reason is that I'm not an academic. I'm not a self-help expert. This is a book based on street smarts, real-life struggles and wins, and a real journey. There are many books out there that can and will add value and give you direction; some may say there are too many! How many books have you started to read but never finished? I often tell people that if I were as smart as all the books

17

on my bookcase, I would be one of the smartest people in the world. But where most books give you theory, I'm going to give you simple, clear, realistic advice that cuts to the chase and can make a positive difference in your life *today*!

Making the Move

For example, a few years ago I was doing some sales training for the Ford Motor Company. I had a session to present in a mid-size regional town called Wagga Wagga approximately mid-way between Sydney and Melbourne. When I arrived, I recognised a guy who had attended one of my presentations some time previously. He came over, shook my hand and said, "G'day, Alex. Remember me? I was in your audience back in Melbourne about 12 months ago when I was working for Nissan." He then went on: "And you know what? The reason I'm here now is you!"

At this point, I wasn't sure whether he was saying this in a positive sense or that I had ruined his life! So I was very glad to hear the rest of his story. He told me that he and his wife had had a house in Melbourne, and they had been talking and dreaming for years about renovating it, selling it and moving to the country, but had been caught up in the Matrix and were worried about giving up their city jobs and taking the plunge. After hearing my presentation, he went home and shared with his wife some of the thinking and philosophies I had shared with him. He said, "Why don't we do this? We could be dead in 10 years." They re-thought their plans, set their goals and acted with new levels of energy and belief. They renovated the house, sold it, quit their jobs and bought a house in the country. They both landed great jobs, and their lives had never been better.

On another occasion, a woman heard one of my presentations and was moved enough to face her fear of the unknown. She went home and told her husband that after tolerating an unhappy marriage for more than 25 years, she was leaving. Now I'm not about breaking up marriages, but I am all about facing reality and making choices that bring you joy and fulfillment.

But the main reason I urge you to reflect on and learn from my story is that I'm walking my talk. There's nothing I'll share with you that I haven't done or not doing myself. I live and die by the principles I share with others. This stuff really does work. I'm living proof of that. It's not always easy... but then again, if it was easy, everyone would be doing it.

I live and die by the principles I share with others. This stuff really does work. I'm living proof of that.

But enough about me. Time to get into the Raw Facts. Thank you for investing your time in what I have to say. I hope you'll find it as challenging, career shifting and life affirming as it's been for me. Let's get started.

If You're Not in the Right Headspace, You're Not Going Anywhere Fast

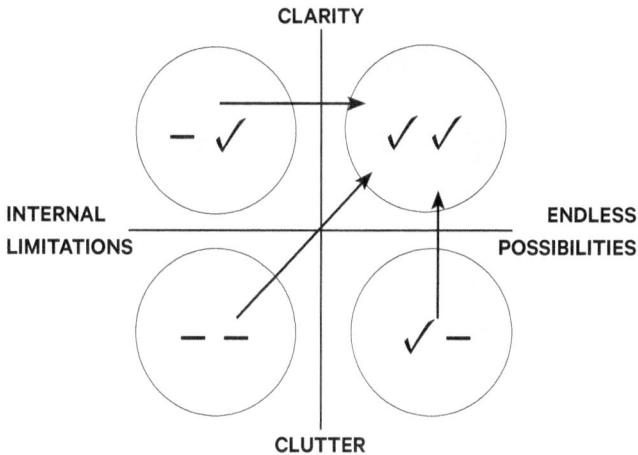

"To see and plan your future, we must first remove our mental clutter and internal limitations."

"The subsistence mentality of a person is a prison in which his personal joy is detained. If you want to live in joy, you don't live for yourself alone. Live for others, too!"

— Israelmore Ayivor, author and motivational speaker

Let's begin with a story. I consider myself to be a motivational speaker with a bucket load of real-life experiences to share. Over the years, I've been honoured and privileged to help thousands of people achieve new levels of accomplishment and fulfillment with their professional and personal lives. I also consider myself to be relatively self-aware and stable. So if someone had told me four years ago that I would be diagnosed with clinical depression and anxiety, be seeing a psychologist, taking antidepressants, spending days in bed in the fetal position and other days at the mercy of uncontrollable crying fits, and even had thoughts of suicide, I would have laughed at them and called them crazy. Well, you just don't know what the universe is going to throw your way and how it will humble you.

Successful people aren't good at acknowledging their weaknesses; we like to pretend that, for us, strength follows strength.

Successful people aren't good at acknowledging their weaknesses; we like to pretend that, for us, strength follows strength. We like to think that we have the world figured out and our flight path is on track, with clear skies and smooth sailing. We feel that we are totally in control and nothing can bring us down. It's shocking to see how a setback can bring our entire existence crashing down.

So it was in 2011 when my marriage fell apart. Cheryle and I had been together for 20 years and married for seven. We had worked hard to achieve many of our goals and were looking forward to enjoying the fruits of our labour in the happy years ahead.

We had spent the past 10 years building a very sucessful jewellery wholesaling business.

At the time, there were no big players in Australia that were wholesaling semi-precious stones and sterling silver. My sister and brother-in-law had been in the business for several years and presented us with an opportunity to act as their agents in the southern states. After a few years, they decided to move to the UK and we bought the business. I saw an opportunity to take it up a notch by developing and implementing a structured business and marketing model. So with a suitcase of jewellery and absolutely no experience or knowledge, but with a vision and a dream, we went on to create one of the country's leading jewellery wholesalers, serving more than 1,400 businesses with annual revenues in the seven figures.

When my relationship with my wife crumbled, I collapsed. I had lost my wife, my best friend and soul mate. My dreams and goals had been shattered, and I later learnt a great deal about the effects of separation anxiety. The next 12 months were the darkest months of my life. The headspace I was in was one of absolute loss and failure. Self-doubt, depression and darkness plagued me. I was, without question, at my absolute lowest point.

Where was my resilience? Where was my perspective? Why was I completely falling apart? Of course, I still had to pull myself together and work, which meant standing in front of audiences and pretending that I had my stuff together. Imagine what it was like to stand in front of people, trying to motivate and inspire them —with the aim of getting a standing ovation and a 10 out of 10 rating — when my world was spinning out of control. It was awful.

On some of those occasions, it took every fibre of my being to keep from breaking down. During some presentations, it was almost as if I was having an out-of-body experience. I knew what I had to share was meaningful, and I could see and hear myself speaking. However, all the time this little devil was sitting on my shoulder, sneering at me: "You're a fraud. Why don't you take your own medicine, Alex?" It was a strange, difficult time.

It's Your Explanation

I knew I couldn't stay in that space; it would only end in grief. After much self-talk, help from a few close friends and my psychologist, Edith, the clouds slowly started to lift. I raised my head and looked beyond the present. I rationalised that it was okay; this was just a setback, a part of learning and life. I wasn't the only one in the world suffering from a broken marriage, and sure as hell there were many people with greater concerns. Day by day, the skies slowly started to clear a little more. My compass started to find its bearings. After many false starts, I gradually pulled myself out of it and moved on with my life. I set my course, retook the controls and with some degree of trepidation and cautiousness, I taxied down the runway for the next exciting leg in my journey.

My compass started to find its bearings. After many false starts, I gradually pulled myself out of it and moved on with my life.

What changed? The answer is the first of our Raw Facts:

If you're not in the right headspace,
you're not going anywhere fast.

The word ***headspace*** can mean different things to different people, but this is part of my definition:

Your headspace is the way you interpret, rationalise,
respond to and react to the things that happen to you.

Ten people having the same experience will interpret the meaning of that experience in 10 different ways, based on their temperament, background, personality and self-esteem. Think about it. When bad things happen, your explanation for them — the story you tell about why this misfortune befell you — can either give you power or render you powerless.

Let's say you've had a heart attack and you're lucky enough to have survived. As you lie in hospital recovering, perhaps you reflect on your family history of heart disease and the randomness of life and death. Maybe you decide it's all up to God. With that fatalistic explanation for your heart attack tucked away inside your headspace, you're likely to conclude that your health is out of your hands, which means you probably won't make the radical lifestyle changes that might prevent a second, possibly fatal, heart attack.

Now, imagine you're in hospital but your explanation for your heart attack — or, if you want it to sound a bit more exotic, your "myocardial infarction"—centres on personal responsibility. You're overweight. You smoke. You don't exercise. Conclusion: whether or not you have a second heart attack will be greatly determined by the choices you make. If you accept the truth, take ownership of the situation, reset your flight plan and check out of hospital in that headspace, you're likely to feel empowered to act. For example, you might quit smoking, start jogging, eat better foods and lose 25 kilos. Your explanation makes all the difference to what you choose to do.

What got me out of the crushing abyss of depression that followed the break-up of my marriage? I decided it was finally time to move on. Basically, I got sick of feeling sorry for myself. I slowly accepted the reality of the situation and realised that if I was to stop behaving like a suicidal character out of French cinema, I had to recreate my headspace. Without knowing it, I followed this four-step process:

1. **Take ownership of the situation.** In the case of my marriage, I accepted that part of its collapse was my responsibility.
2. **Take stock of the present.** What damage has occurred and how can it be repaired? What positives do you have to work with, and what have you learnt from the experience?

25

3. **Define your purpose and passion.** Why do you do what you do? What do you have to live for?

4. **Redesign your goals.** The past is past. Your goals may be obsolete. What do you strive for moving forward? What are your new goals?

Step One: I stopped feeling sorry for myself. I accepted the situation and stopped blaming others, especially my wife. That was liberating.

Step Two: I looked around at what I had, good and bad, worked hard to remove emotion from my decisions and found that things could have been a lot worse. I had managed to keep my cyclone of emotions out of sight, for the most part. My speaking engagements and consulting practice were going well, and I was still able to work with my ex-wife to exit our jewellery business without destroying it. On the whole, there were a great deal more positives than negatives. For a start, I was alive!

Step Three: I had been in a numb state, simply existing. I had to find motivation and energy. I opened my mind to what was possible and started to rethink what excited me. I needed to find a "Why" to live for. Finally, I did, and it was as though the heavens opened and the sun shone upon me. My purpose was helping and teaching others!

Step Four: I changed my goals. Before our breakup, my intent was to semi-retire at age 55, book the occasional speaking engagement, have my investment properties for a stream of income and tour around Australia in a luxury caravan, becoming one of those "grey nomads" who spend half the year in the Top End of Australia fishing for barramundi and mud crabs. I would wear shirts with insufferably loud patterns and become an expert in the fine wines of the Barossa Valley. It seemed perfect.

After I climbed out of my dark place, everything changed. Deep down, I still had my travel and leisure plans, but my attention turned to helping people who were in the position I had been. I had (and have) a much greater appreciation for mental health issues, such as clinical depression. That helped me put together presentations for people enduring the same kind of horror show I'd lived through.

Asking Why

Earlier, I said that how we explain things that happen to us is *part* of the definition of headspace. What's the other part? It comes down to a question: *Why?* Taking control of your headspace is also about understanding why you do what you do. You may think you know, but as Simon Sinek wrote in his bestselling book, *Start With Why,* "You have to be careful with what you think you know."

The question of why brings up the metaphor that inspired the title of this book. The way I see it, you can either be the 'Pilot' on your journey through life or a 'Passenger'.

The question of why brings up the metaphor that inspired the title of this book. The way I see it, you can either be the 'Pilot' on your journey through life or a 'Passenger'.

Why do you get up each day and go through the same rituals and routines? Do you know the reason, or do you do them unconsciously? Research shows that in developed countries, between 70 and 80 per cent of employees dislike their jobs. About one-third of employees consider themselves emotionally detached from their employer and do just enough to avoid being sacked. Another third drag themselves to work unmotivated and disengaged, and I think that's a very sad place to be.

I often ask this question of my audiences: *"Why do you do what you do?"* Why do you get up early six or seven days a week, get ready for work, head off into traffic, spend the next eight or 10 hours at work, then head back home only to do it all again the following day, week after week, year after year? Most people avoid the obvious truth, and it takes some coaxing to get them to be honest and admit that they do what they do for the money. Not because they love their work or love the people they work with. They work because they have to; most people do.

With such a large percentage of workers feeling unhappy, unmotivated and disengaged, then the main reason they're working is to pay the bills. Don't get me wrong; money is important. Even if you love what you do, loving the work is not enough. You need to be compensated. If your employer or clients were unable to pay you, and even if you love your job, you would eventually have to find another job or new clients, otherwise you would starve.

Money is important. Money gives us choices. Money allows us to pursue and enjoy the lifestyle we want. Money also gives us the opportunity to help others. I've had money and I've had no money – sound familiar? And, believe me, having money is bucket loads better than having no money. Some people say having no money builds character. I say, hang character! Having money is better that having to eat the bark off trees to survive.

When money becomes your reason for doing what you do, then you have a problem. Money is the outcome of work; it's never the reason or purpose behind work.

When money becomes your **reason** for doing what you do, then you have a problem. Money should be the outcome of work; not the **reason** or **purpose** for work.

To help you with your goals and aspirations, look at work through this perspective:

*Your career is the vehicle for generating income to invest
or build something with, in order to create the wealth
you will need to live the future lifestyle you want.*

Re-read that a few times and think about it. From that perspective, it makes sense that the better you are at what you do, the more success you will enjoy. You will make more money, create more wealth and have more freedom to create the lifestyle of your dreams. So it's in your best interest to be the best you can be! Learn, grow, focus, model – whatever it takes. But in the end, in order to bring perspective, enjoyment and motivation into your world, you must find the meaning and purpose behind your career. If you can't, perhaps it's time for a new career.

Punching Through the Clouds

Human beings are motivated by meaning and purpose; money is just a tool. Tools don't have meaning or purpose. They're transactional; you employ Tool A in order to produce Result B. Transaction concluded, here's your change, have a lovely day. If money is your "why", then you could be living a life devoid of meaning or purpose, and no person can live that way.

Many people live lives of unconscious, self-imposed obligation, tippy-toeing through life safely to death, conditioned from childhood by family, friends and the media.

Many people live lives of unconscious, self-imposed obligation, tippy-toeing through life safely to death, conditioned from childhood by family, friends and the media. We don't like to talk about money, but we find ourselves doing things for money without questioning whether those things are giving us what we really want. That gives rise to an even more important question:

Where are you heading? What do you really want and why?

Popular culture and the system expect that you will keep your head down, keep quiet and go on feeding the hours and months and years of your life into the Matrix — leading what Henry David Thoreau called a life of "quiet desperation". But what if you stuck your head up and looked around? I call it "popping". It's like taking your jet out of auto-pilot, pulling the stick back and punching it through the clouds into the bright sunshine.

Every now and again, someone realises that there's more to life, that there just might be a better way, and they want to know and achieve more. They pop their head up and realise they have the power to break free of unconscious living and everyone's expectations, and start living deliberately and intentionally. You need to start asking:

- Is what I'm doing today getting me closer to what I want?
- If not, why am I doing what I'm doing?
- If yes, what can I do to get there faster?
- What do I need to change and how can I do it?

The people who can't or won't ask these questions are Passengers. They will never have full control over where they're going — and many don't want to take control. It's so much easier being a Passenger, right? The people who ask those questions again and again are conscious of the moment and will find the answers. They are the **Pilots**.

They are in control of their headspace, aware of their bearings and have a clear picture of where they are going. They're in charge of their journey. They are mindful, living consciously and deliberately, fully aware of the reasons behind their choices. They're always fine tuning, making adjustments to keep on track and never afraid to change course to a new and more exciting destination. If you're a

Passenger, this book is about turning you into a Pilot. If you're already a Pilot, this book is about making you a better one.

Years ago, I was enjoying a wonderful conversation with a senior commercial pilot, who had more than 10,000 hours of flying time, about the metaphor of "Pilot or Passenger". He said to me, "Life is just like flying a jet — the day you think there's no more to learn or you take your eye off the ball is the day you will crash and burn."

> *"Life is just like flying a jet — the day you think there's no more to learn is the day you will crash and burn."*

Changing Your Headspace

Becoming the Pilot of your life's journey starts with examining and recalibrating your headspace. Think of it as giving yourself, in the words of Zig Ziglar, a "checkup from the neck up". Think of your headspace as the navigational compass in your heart and head. If it's adjusted properly, you'll go where you want to go: to a life of meaning, fulfillment, joy and achievement. But if it's calibrated to accept complacency, unconsciously conform or to have negative feelings such as guilt or anger, then you will probably look up from the grindstone in 25 years and wonder, "Where the hell am I and how did I get here?" Or you'll be saying to yourself and everyone around you that "life sucks".

To calibrate that internal compass correctly, you need four essential tools—four cornerstones to use as the foundations of your mind:

1. A Positive Attitude
2. Vision
3. Self-Belief
4. Focus

1. Positive Attitude

In the 1990s, I was fortunate enough to be selected to go on a two-week study tour in the US. Unfortunately, the weather was awful. I didn't see the sun the entire time. It was depressing. But when I flew from city to city, we would pop through and fly above the clouds, and the brilliance of blue sky and sunshine was breathtaking. That was the birth of one of my favourite sayings: "The sun is always shining above the clouds."

However, as we know, Mother Nature is not going to bathe us in fine weather and sunshine for our entire life's journey. From time to time, we all face storms and squalls that have the potential to bring us down. When we're unhappy, it's easy to only see the grey clouds and get caught in negativity and defeatism. We start to feel that it's all too much or too hard, and that it would be so much easier to be a Passenger and accept our lot, even if it's not close to where we dream of going. We start to give in to "I can't" thinking: *I can't change things. I can't change jobs. I can't go back to studying. I can't just sell my house and relocate.* That kind of relentless negativity will suck the life out of everything you try to do. A negative attitude becomes negative self-talk, and soon you'll convince yourself that you can't do anything. That's what psychologists call "learned helplessness".

A negative attitude becomes negative self-talk, and soon you'll convince yourself that you can't do anything. That's what psychologists call "learned helplessness".

I'm not going to tell you to simply put on a happy face, because that's not realistic. If you've spent decades being pessimistic, for me to say, "Just look on the bright side," is as insensitive as somebody telling a person suffering with depression to "get over it". But there is a way to reboot your attitude in a more positive way: changing your perspective.

First recognise the power of becoming a "realistic optimist". Look at the familiar from a different aspect or position. For example, it's easy to plot our position on Earth. We can pinpoint our exact position by using the points of a compass (or switching on our GPS). However, you can't do this in space. The directions of the compass are meaningless. This is where *attitude* comes into play.

In space, astronauts plot their position and flight paths using attitude — their position relative to celestial objects, such as stars and planets. Before and during a mission, astronauts carefully plot the spacecraft's course and map the locations of bodies whose gravitational forces will affect its trajectory. Navigators must also keep in mind that everything is moving. The spacecraft is traveling thousands of kilometres per hour. The Earth is rotating and moving around the Sun, which is also moving.

In moving through our world towards our goals, we're like the spacecraft. Many forces can affect our course and some can throw us off course. Your *attitude* is your position relative to the other things in your world. How you navigate through them will determine where you end up. But you can't blindly navigate on autopilot. You have to look at your world from a different position, become aware of your surroundings and your *attitude*. Then you may start to see things in a different light.

How can you reset your attitude? Get things in perspective. We get so caught up in what we see as our misfortune — "someone else got the job I wanted; his life is perfect but mine's always hard" — that we forget our world is not *the* world. Reach out and help others who are less fortunate: volunteer at a homeless shelter, visit people in hospitals and nursing homes, or read to kids who don't have parents to read to them. You'll see that your problems aren't so huge after all. This is a wonderful way to get a reality check and a

33

fresh perspective. It frees us from the Matrix and reveals the depth of our conditioning.

If you think you have problems or you're not happy with the way things are in your life, step back and have a good look at what's around you physically, spiritually and emotionally.

If you think you have problems or you're not happy with the way things are in your life, step back and have a good look at what's around you physically, spiritually and emotionally. Spare a thought for the thousands of adults and children around the world in hospitals, burn units and cancer wards. Think about the millions of people who don't have enough to eat. Think about the people around the world who have nothing and still manage to smile.

I have visited India on a number of occasions and it's always a reality check for me. There is a particular intersection in Jaipur where a crippled mother and her three children, all under the age of seven, have claimed the first four meters of a concrete median strip just over a metre wide. They live there under a collection of cardboard boxes and are covered in rags. As the traffic stops, the children reach up to the car windows with pleading eyes and cupped hands, gesturing for food or money. I have observed this family for the past few years and what humbles me and brings tears to my eyes are the beaming smiles on these children's faces. They are the very picture of poverty, yet they always wear an infectious smile.

So before you complain that your coffee was too hot or too cold, so-and-so got the promotion you thought you deserved, or the stock market fell 2 per cent, stop. Think about how blessed you really are. You're alive, mindful and have choices. It could be very different. It was for my best friend, Steve "Macca", a couple of years ago. Macca was attending a wedding in a village high in the mountains of Vietnam. He was only 58, had recently retired and was loving it. But on the night of the wedding, he suffered a heart attack and with no medical assistance available, he died. Had it happened in a different time, in a different place, Macca might still be with us today. I really miss him.

Things aren't so bad in your world. The future isn't so hopeless. You're not such a muck-up. In fact, if people suffering from poverty, hunger, homelessness or addiction can face their lives with a positive attitude, why shouldn't you? A fresh perspective shows you the way things really are — it makes the sun come out from behind the clouds.

2. Vision

Throughout my journey, I have found the power of visualisation fundamental to my motivation. Firstly, you need to have a mental picture of what can be. What do you want to achieve? What's your destination? Dream it, see it, desire it and make it happen.

When you go to a travel agent, you are surrounded by glossy brochures of beautiful destinations. They are there to tempt you to dream, desire and make a decision. Life's journey is no different. Close your eyes and see what you want your future to look like.

3. Belief

Beliefs are the operating system of the mind. They purr along beneath conscious thoughts and emotions. Basically, beliefs define three things:

1. The kind of person you are.
2. The world you live in.
3. How you interact with that world.

But the most important fact about beliefs is this: *you will never accomplish more than your beliefs allow you to*. While it's possible with coaching and training to exceed your potential in areas such as academics or athletics, you will never exceed what you believe to be impossible. To have the kind of life and career you can love, you've got to believe you have what it takes to achieve your goals. Another way to put it is; Until you change your beliefs, the emotions, thoughts and actions that reside above them cannot change.

"Whether you think you can or think you can't, you're right."

—Henry Ford

The trouble is that there will always (and I mean *always*) be a group of people who simply will not believe that something is possible until it happens — and then some still doggedly challenge the result or outcome because they can't accept a new belief, or accept they were wrong.

*The trouble is that there will always (and I mean **always**) be a group of people who simply will not believe that something is possible until it happens...*

Does the name Roger Bannister mean anything to you? If you're a distance runner, I'll bet it does. Back in 1954, he became famous by being the first person in the world to run a mile in under four minutes. Before he ran his historic mile, it was widely believed it just wasn't possible. Some medical experts insisted that the human body was not capable of such a feat. Then, on the 6th of May 1954, Bannister did it. Within a month, other runners had broken the four-minute barrier as well. It was as though Roger Bannister had granted the entire running world permission to believe in itself.

The lesson of Roger Bannister's four-minute mile is that you will always encounter doubters. If you listen to them, you give them power. That's okay. Everyone is entitled to his or her own opinions and beliefs. But remember who is telling you what and why they may have formed their beliefs. Also remember the people who try to block you or tear you down are almost always doing so because they are afraid to take a risk themselves. If you tell yourself something is impossible, you are giving yourself an excuse not to try, and if you don't try you can't fail.

There is safety and comfort in numbers, so it's much easier to go with the majority rather than step up. These people fear that your success will make them feel regret and humiliation. Others will insist you were lucky or that their failure is someone else's fault. All you can do is resist their negativity and believe in yourself!

The fact is, it doesn't matter what family you were born into or what school you went to. If you want to believe in yourself, you must get rid of your negative beliefs. Catch every negative thought that comes into your mind and spit it out! Reinvent your belief system by finding new, positive examples or role models who are achieving exactly what want to achieve. Show your brain that it's possible. Get new points of reference to what is achievable: "If they can, so can I!"

When I was rebooting my life, I started telling myself: "I'm going to achieve this! I don't know how I'm going to do it but I'm going to achieve it!" That triggered my brain to constantly look for ways to turn my thoughts into reality.

Do you want to tear down the longstanding belief that you're not good enough or smart enough? Deliver an open challenge to your limiting belief: What's the evidence that you're not good enough? Is there any evidence? When you ask that question honestly, you may find that the answer is: "No." Okay, you may have tried something and it didn't work — big deal! Think, assess, learn, modify and try again and again until you succeed!

Another way to challenge and change limiting beliefs is to take risks. Risk is the fuel of change and, as in finance, the greater the risk, the greater the reward. Nothing will transform your perception of your own capacity than sticking your neck out, trying something you've never done before, and achieving some success at it — even if that success is partial.

Risk is the fuel of change and, as in finance, the greater the risk, the greater the reward.

For example: My friends Mary and Jeff had never owned a boat and were not boating people. They had never owned so much as a 10-foot aluminium fishing punt, and the only time they had been on the water was on a South Pacific cruise and a camping weekend with a canoe. Then one day, they happened to be at a conference in Sydney and there was a boat show on the harbour. During his free afternoon, Jeff slipped down to the show and fell in love with a million-dollar yacht. I mean, he fell head over heels in love; he thought it was the duck's guts. Jeff spent three or four hours with the boat's designer and builder, and a dream was born.

The next day, he and Mary hatched a borderline-insane scheme: with zero sailing experience, they were going to pay a deposit, order the yacht, and in a year they would take delivery and sail around Australia.

When they told me about their plans, I said (with what I thought was admirable restraint), "Wow. That's awesome!" But I felt a low-grade panic building for my friends. I'm a boater and I don't particularly like the idea of being a tiny little speck in the middle of the Pacific Ocean on a dark and stormy night. But not wanting to rain on their parade, I simply asked, "So guys, what's your game plan?" Their answer didn't surprise me. Jeff simply said, "Other people do it all the time. Even 16-year-olds have sailed around the world solo. If they can do it, so can we. We just have to learn how to do it!"

Jeff and Mary's belief system said, "We can learn to sail," so they joined the local yacht club and took a year and a half to learn about sailing, seamanship, boat maintenance and navigation, which was perfect because there was a delay with the delivery of their yacht. Finally, two years after the genesis of their dream, they headed off on the adventure of their lives and spent the next two years sailing around Australia.

You don't have to sail around the world, but if you want to give your beliefs about yourself a shot of adrenaline, try something that tests you.

You don't have to sail around the world, but if you want to give your beliefs about yourself a shot of adrenaline, try something that tests you.

Focused But Flexible

Once you have a positive attitude and a rebooted sense of belief, you're ready for the third part of a healthy headspace: a laser focus on what you want.

It's easy to get distracted, to fall into the trap of drifting into the numbing comfort of being a Passenger in the back of the plane on the mystery flight of life. You don't have to plan, set bearings — hell, you don't even have to think. But then you don't have any control over where your Pilot is taking you. He may love the snow in the Swiss Alps, while you think you're heading to a sunny beach in tropical Fiji. Somebody's going to be disappointed. To arrive at *your* destination of choice, you need to stay focused and in control,

*To arrive at **your** destination of choice, you need to stay focused and in control, and that means being in that Pilot's seat.*

and that means being in that Pilot's seat.

Part of the problem is that our entire civilisation is trying to break our focus. In 2001, I read a Stanford University study that said we were exposed to more than 3,500 commercial messages every day. When I read that figure, I thought, "No way." But then it went on to explain that commercial messages are insidious: they flash before our eyes and attack our senses in all manner of ways. Take, for example, driving to work. Every car you pass has a brand logo on it. Bingo! Commercial message. As you drive past a strip of shops, you see another 50 or 100 messages. Walk down a supermarket aisle and notice how many brands and labels there are. Add radio, television, periodicals, opinions from friends, family and colleagues, and even household objects — the pen you write with probably has a brand message on it — and it's a wonder we can think at all!

Mental Clutter – The Enemy of Focus

After I read that, the idea of 3,500 messages became very real. That was 14 years ago, before the internet, Google, Facebook, Twitter, laptops, tablets and smart phones! I'd guess that today, we're probably exposed to more than ***ten thousand*** commercial messages a day, most of them barely registering with our conscious mind. But they all add up to outrageous mental clutter.

Fortunately, our brains generally only register what is of interest or importance to us. For example, if you are into camping, you would have noticed the camping store on the way to your office. If you're not into camping, you've probably never given it a second thought. Another instance that you're probably familiar with is when you've just bought a new car and suddenly you see hundreds of cars that are the same make, model and colour as the one you just bought. Where did they come from? They were always there; you're just noticing them because now they're relevant to you. They have a purchase on your attention – they're on your radar.

The world bombards us with mental clutter: sights, sounds, the internet and a million meaningless distractions. They're part of the brainwashing, conditioning and propaganda that tell us what to think, buy, say and do. They tell us we should stop asking questions, keep our heads down and work so that we can get another loan or credit card to buy the latest car, smartphone or television. Once you block the propaganda out, it's like waking up. Your headspace begins to change.

> *The world bombards us with mental clutter: sights, sounds, the internet and a million meaningless distractions … once you block the propaganda out, it's like waking up. Your headspace begins to change.*

The deaths of Andrew's wife and Keven, the new account manager at Finemores, were my wake-up calls. My illness and Macca's death were reminders. Up to that point, my focus had been on climbing the corporate ladder. I wanted to be the best cadet, the best manager, to develop the best convenience stores, build the best chain and have the best franchises. I was obsessed with producing results. It wasn't about the money; I've always figured that when you only focus on money, things go pear-shaped quickly. Focus on doing things right and money inevitably follows. And doing things right comes from the inner you.

Still, my obsession was with the process. I didn't realise what it was costing me. When I stepped back and expanded my field of view, what I saw stunned me. I saw a pyramid with layers. At the base is a world crowded with Passengers checked in to mystery flights with standard, barely comfortable discount seats. Many are unaware of their unhappiness and simply accept the varying degrees of service. The collective echo is, "Well, there's no point complaining, nobody ever listens."

But as I looked higher, the pyramid wasn't as crowded. There were more planes than people and people were happier. They were in control of their space and their journey. Most importantly, most of these people were guiding other people to planes that were waiting for Pilots. There are a lot of people ready to help you climb into the Pilot's seat. The problem is, you won't see these opportunities to pursue meaning and change if you go through life with your head down.

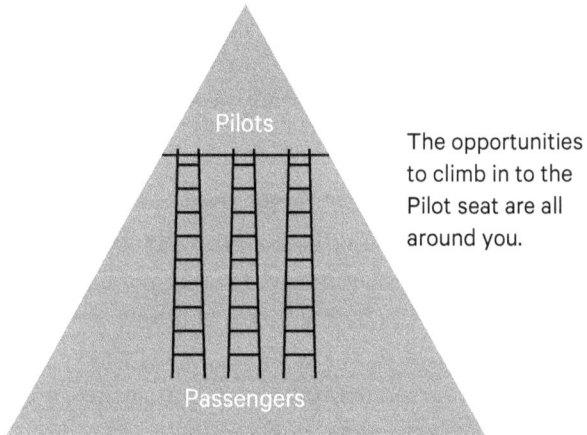

The opportunities to climb in to the Pilot seat are all around you.

Other times, people see the air stairs leading to that open cockpit, but ignore them because of fear: fear of the unknown, fear of failure, fear of "popping" out of their comfort zone, of having to leave their friends and families behind.

Once I changed my focus, I saw opportunities everywhere; chances for me to sit in the Pilot's seat and take the controls. I was able to own my space and refocus my mind on what I wanted to achieve.

The Headspace Process

There's an old and well-proven process that's highly effective at reprogramming your headspace. I use it all the time and it requires answers to these four questions:

1. What did you learn while getting to where you are today?
2. Where is here? What does it mean to be where you are?
3. Where do you want to go next?
4. How will you use what you've learned to get there?

This is *intentional* living. When we settle for being Passengers and let ourselves be brainwashed by the barrage of commercial messages, we live unconsciously. Take control of where your attention goes and you become a Pilot. Grabbing the ladders that appear in your life is the first step to doing that. Grasp the opportunities with both hands, take the controls and reset your bearings and course. Know that you have the right to do this — that you *deserve* to do it. It's liberating.

Once you know what you want, lock it in. Set the coordinates. Find others who are already doing it and learn how they got there. Do the research, find out how they did it, talk to them and ask them. Remember, the overwhelming majority of successful people are more than happy to share their knowledge and experience to teach you to fly.

Remember, the overwhelming majority of successful people are more than happy to share their knowledge and experience to teach you to fly.

43

Write your goals, and rewrite them daily —or at least read them daily. Stamp them deep into your brain cells and visualise the joy of the achievements you strive for. Keep them top of mind.

Finally, resist any temptation to pull your mind away from the pursuit of what you want. Ignore the calls from society, friends or family trying to pull you back to the comforting numbness of an unconscious existence.

Actually, I don't think that will be a problem. After you have a new attitude, a revised belief system and a laser focus on your goals, your previous conditioning won't hold any appeal. You'll have a new headspace oriented to the kind of life you can celebrate.

Key Questions

We're being conditioned every day to follow rules, buy this, want that and not speak up. When papers say the stock market is on shaky ground, retail sales fall. When the media tells us the economy is good, people feel wealthier and spend more. Every message you receive, everything you read, everything you hear and see has the potential to influence you and alter your thinking and belief system. My mentor, Bob, used to say, "AB, paper doesn't refuse ink"— meaning everything you read isn't necessarily true. What you're exposed to will have an effect on you, but if you look at who's writing the message and its intent, you can control its effect. Become the gatekeeper of your mind and keep out the garbage.

Let's ask some hard questions:

- Awareness: How am I being negatively conditioned?
- Why and how is it happening?
- Who and what is conditioning me?
- What impact is this conditioning having on my attitude, beliefs and focus?

- What will it mean if I reject that conditioning?
- What changes do I need to make to achieve my goals?

Then you can move on to the really tough questions:

- What do I want from my life and why?
- How is my present situation preventing me from having that life?
- What part of my current situation is my responsibility?
- How can I take stock of my present situation?
- What are my new goals?
- Is my attitude tilted towards the positive or negative? Why?
- What do I believe I am capable of doing?
- What is that belief based on?
- Where is my attention focused and how must my focus change?

The Million-Dollar Question

*Where does my headspace need to be in order
to get what I want most from life?*

To Know What's Next, Know Your Gap

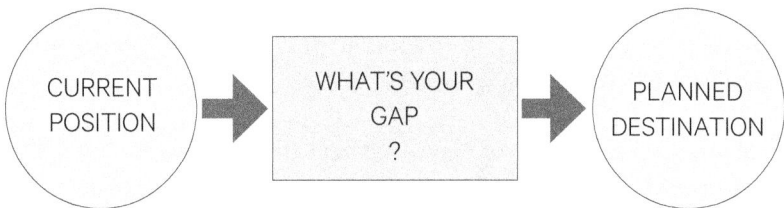

| CURRENT POSITION | → | WHAT'S YOUR GAP ? | → | PLANNED DESTINATION |

"...dare to dream and imagine what could be ... then work on bridging the gap."

"If there is dissatisfaction with the status quo, good. If there is ferment, so much the better. If there is restlessness, I am pleased. Then let there be ideas, and hard thought, and hard work. If man feels small, let man make himself bigger."

—Hubert H. Humphrey

Most people, if they are honest with themselves, would agree that there is a gap between where they are now and where they would like to be.

Most people, if they are honest with themselves, would agree that there is a gap between where they are now and where they would like to be. There are periods in our lives when the gap is small; at other times, it can seem an unbridgeable chasm. Before we can start working towards bridging the gap, we must first recognise that we *have* a gap. Now that we've talked about adopting a positive mindset, realising what is possible and seeing the boundless opportunities that surround us, it's time to look at the question: "Where am I now and where do I want to be?"

Having a clear vision of this is critical to your future. Take the example of Chris "Macca" McCormack, an Australian triathlete and one of the greatest champions in the history of triathlon. In 2010, at age 37, he became the oldest athlete in history to win the fabled Ironman Triathlon in Hawaii. But in his book, *I'm Here to Win*, he wrote that his career almost never started. Because when he was 22, Chris McCormack, one of the greatest endurance athletes of all time, was an accountant.

His story is classic: he hungered to compete on the European triathlon circuit but his parents, worried that their son would wind up impoverished, pressed him to get an accounting degree and take a desk job. Chris did – and he hated every second of it. He worried that if he didn't take a risk and try to earn a spot on a European team, he would regret it for the rest of his life. His drive became so ferocious that he eventually quit his job, but neglected to inform his parents.

Each day, his father would drive him to the train station in their Sydney suburb, thinking that Chris was going to work. But after his father drove away, Chris would change into his running gear and spend the day training. At day's end, he would clean up, change back into his business suit, and meet his father at the train station, telling him about his "day at the office". Eventually, of course, the young man came clean. He told his father and mother what he had done, sold all his possessions and bought a ticket to Europe on an all-or-nothing mission to become a professional triathlete. The rest is racing history.

Tiptoeing Through Life Safely to Death

Chris McCormack did three critical things in the early stages of his path to a legendary athletic career: he arrived at the proper headspace, he believed in himself and he clearly saw the gap between where he was and where he wanted to be. Instinctively, he already understood the Raw Fact for this chapter:

To know what's next, you have to know your gap.

Life is like a dance, and we're constantly evolving and moving to keep up with the music as it changes. If you're static, you're already pushing up daisies. The trouble is, there are lots of people — maybe even you — who are living as though they've already shuffled off this mortal coil. What do I mean? Well, they've accepted that where they are today is where they are going to stay for the rest of their lives. They don't even look around to see the better future that might be well within their reach.

Life is like a dance, and we're constantly evolving and moving to keep up with the music as it changes.

The difference between where you are today and where you want to be in two, five or 10 years is your gap. Identifying your gap is critical to having the life and career you want. On the other side of

49

your gap is your destination; you're like Indiana Jones looking across the chasm when the rickety rope bridge is down. The treasure is on the other side. How are you going to get there? That's the question, and careful planning and action are the answer. But until you look up, see the gap and decide the other side is where you want to be, you're simply existing. You're a Passenger with no control over what happens tomorrow. As we've already discussed, if you want to have the life of your dreams, you must take charge and be the Pilot of your life.

If you want to have the life of your dreams, you must take charge and be the Pilot of your life.

Chris McCormack saw his gap. On one side of the chasm was his life as an accountant, working a nine-to-five job in a cubicle for the next 30 years. There's nothing wrong with being an accountant, but it wasn't the right life for *him*. On the other side was his dream of being a professional triathlete. Seeing that gap and knowing that he simply had to bridge it was the motivating force that led him to quit his job, sell everything he owned and risk everything to chase his dream.

Having a gap is healthy. It means you aspire to something. You're not "tiptoeing through life safely to death". People who do that make only safe choices, live as society expects them to live, and never look beyond the borders of their predictable lives. They may not make any grievous mistakes, but they also don't achieve anything extraordinary. World-changing entrepreneurs, great inventors, brilliant artists and achievers don't tiptoe through life. They stomp, they strut, they dance. They look for and create gaps, setting themselves new goals and challenges while taking action to bridge those gaps and achieve their new goals.

I'm sure you have known people who were unable, for various reasons, to recognise that they had a gap, let alone bridge it. Perhaps they were too fearful to really live, or they were stuck in a rut, convinced that this was their lot and that life was tolerable. Perhaps they had been the victims of bad luck. What were these people like?

If they were like some people I've known, they were bitter, frustrated and hopeless. I've known people who, despite their unhappiness, habitually said things such as: "It's just the way it is," and, "No point having dreams, no fairy's going to make my wishes come true." They had totally disempowered themselves; they were Passengers for life. They felt helpless to change things and remained trapped in their situations. Some of them probably drank or took drugs to numb their pain. Being unable to escape a life you feel is smothering you leaves you in a negative, dark headspace, and it can be easy to end up there.

You don't want to be that person. If you did, you wouldn't be reading this book, right? So let's talk about how you can: a) identify your gap, and b) figure out the first steps to bridge it.

The Adaptation Principle

It's the early part of the last century, and a dusty prospector rides his horse into an outback town from one of the gold fields of Western Australia. Reaching the pub, he ties his horse to a hitching post and walks inside for some well-earned beers. A few minutes later, another prospector rides up on his horse. But this horse is so laden with gear that his back is bowed, his belly almost touching the ground.

This second prospector ties his horse outside and walks into the pub. The first horse turns to the bow-backed horse and says, "Mate, how do you manage with that enormous load?"

The second horse looks puzzled and replies, "What load?"

That's the *adaptation principle* in action. Basically, it says that we quickly become used to our current state, whatever it is. Good or bad, we adapt to it and it becomes our new normal. If you aspire to something better and have trained yourself to savour risks and push your boundaries, the adaptation principle will make you feel dissatisfied with what you have. You will be restless to do better, live better, have more and explore your potential. The adaptation principle is a positive force in your life.

If you aspire to something better and have trained yourself to savour risks and push your boundaries, the adaptation principle will make you feel dissatisfied with what you have.

If, on the other hand, your tendency is to settle for where you are, to fear risk and to not challenge the status quo, the adaptation principle will make you comfortable with suboptimal circumstances — an unfulfilling job, an unhealthy relationship, and so on. You'll accept what you have and won't even think to question the load on your back that makes your belly touch the ground. You'll be another drone mindlessly riding the train each day to a job you don't even realise you hate.

You know people like that. We all do. They've buried their inner child. What do I mean? Think about what it was like when you were young. The first five years of life are fantastic! Everything is great. Everything is exciting. We laughed, we cried, and we could do anything. When you're five, everything is possible. You can drink toilet water and eat cat poo and go back for more, and everyone is a new best friend. Right?

From birth throughout childhood, we are like sponges. Our brains take in massive amounts of information. We are curious about everything. Every second word is "Why?" We want to know and understand everything and we use all our senses – it's great! But then things start to change. We start school and some teachers teach us how *not* to learn. Remarks such as, "That's a silly question, Alex", or, "Just sit and be quiet or you will be in trouble!" filled our ears (they certainly did mine). We learn to conform and be self-conscious. We learn about embarrassment and we hate looking stupid. We learn that praise feels good and being berated makes us feel bad, so we learn to blend in and go with the flow and stop asking questions.

As time goes on, other people continue to influence and shape our belief systems. They plant seeds in our minds. Many people today are living lives that other people seeded for them years ago. Comments such as, "Johnny, you're hopeless at math, you'll never be an accountant," or,

As time goes on, other people continue to influence and shape our belief systems.

"Mary, loves plaiting her doll's hair, she's going to be a hairdresser when she grows up," can eventually become beliefs and manifest into actions.

Then we leave school and get a job. Remember how exciting it was when you got your first job, how proud you were? You couldn't wait to tell your family and friends. But JOB stands for Just Over Broke. A job is designed to be a stepping stone to something better, not a lifestyle. When you have a job, you get paid just enough on Friday so that you have to come back on Monday.

When you have a *career*, you have purpose, connection and commitment. Remember, your career is the vehicle you have chosen to generate the income, to create the wealth that you'll need to live the lifestyle you want in the future. So, ask yourself: do you have a 'job' or a 'career'? They're different circumstances and they reflect completely different mindsets.

At some point along your journey, you meet someone and fall in love. It's exciting! The heart flutters and you're walking on clouds ... until you surrender to more unconscious expectations. You get married, buy a house and make babies. Then you meet someone else, and have to buy another one (sorry, that's just my twisted sense of humour). Along the way, you hopefully have a few good holidays, maybe buy a new car or two, and when you hit 65, you retire. After that, you spend 20 years pottering about, thinking of all the things you *should have* done and *could have* done ... and then you fall off the perch! Game over.

I'll bet that 80 per cent of people are being conditioned from childhood to follow exactly that path without ever questioning it — to tippy-toe through life safely to death. It's a life philosophy that encourages us to settle, to accept mediocrity. A philosophy that's perpetuated through our politics, governments and religion, because the last thing a government wants is a population of thinking, aspiring, questioning people.

By the time many of us realise we've been conditioned, we feel it's too late or too hard to change.

Today, many people are living lives seeded in their minds by other people. *Study hard. Get a good job. Security is important.* By the time many of us realise we've been conditioned, we feel it's too late or too hard to change.

Stop and take stock of the career path you're on. Is the vehicle you've chosen a lean, mean, prosperity-creating machine? If it's not, then there's your gap. It's time to embrace it and go about crossing it before it's too late.

Your True Level of Dissatisfaction

Over the years, I had consciously and subconsciously identified and bridged gaps in my life that stood between where I was and where I wanted to be. Four years ago, I thought my gap was relatively small. Life was going along nicely, or so I thought. I had goals and plans, had built my business, made my semi-retirement plans, arranged fishing trips and long-term holidays. The planets were aligning and I was starting to enjoy the fruits of my labour. Then, in a heartbeat, separation and divorce turned those plans to ash.

Before this happened, if you had asked me what my gap was, I would have told you that it was small. It certainly wasn't the same as it is now. I thought I was where I wanted to be. However, about two years after everything fell apart, I took stock and realised something that astonished me: I was actually starting from a better mental and emotional position than the one I was in when I was married.

I also saw that I had been lying to myself for years. Ever so slowly, little frustrations had been building in my world: family and personal issues, business frustrations and more. I had been suppressing them, choosing to ignore them, which is a big mistake. By ignoring small irritations, I'd slowly veered off course by convincing myself that I was still heading in the right direction. Eventually, I paid the price. Don't make the same mistake. Shed the crap and don't harbour the little things that can blind you to the gap in your life.

The truly heavy lifting in bridging the gap between today and tomorrow lies in being totally honest with yourself and *seeing that you have a gap in the first place*. It's easy to allow mediocrity — that feeling of good enough — to lull us into complacency. When we make

> *It's easy to allow mediocrity — that feeling of good enough — to lull us into complacency.*

55

excuses for the nagging anxiety we have about going into work, when we mock those who've had the courage to chase their dreams, when we ignore the longing in our stomachs when we see that path we wish we'd taken but didn't, we're living in complacency. It can be fatal. Ignore the signs or your intuition, your gut feeling, and the results can be catastrophic.

However, the beauty of life is that we have choices. I could have chosen to blame the universe and the horrible hand I was dealt and feel sorry for myself. If I had, odds are I'd still be doing exactly that today. My other choice was to take stock, say, "If it's to be, it's up to me," realign my dreams and desires, and take a hard, honest look at my gap. How far was the distance between where I was four years ago and where I wanted to be in one, two, five years and beyond?

The secret to discovering the scope and nature of your gap is finding your true levels of desire and dissatisfaction.

The fact is, there's always a gap. No one has everything they want. But it's a matter of degrees. Sometimes, all you need to do is slap a coat of fresh paint on your life and call it good. Other times, you need a full knock down and rebuild, to tear the whole structure down and rebuild from the foundations up. The secret to discovering the scope and nature of your gap is finding your *true levels of desire and dissatisfaction.*

I often use the analogy of people being like a dog lying on a stone. You'll see a dog lying in the sun, stretched out, eyes closed, blissfully asleep. But every now and again he'll shuffle and make a little "humph" sound as he wiggles to get comfortable. Turns out, he's lying on a little stone and it's digging into his ribs. It's not quite uncomfortable enough to make him get up and move, but annoying enough to disrupt his nap. He'll tolerate it until the discomfort finally forces him to get up and move.

Some people are the same. They'll bitch and whine and huff and puff and complain about the stone that's sticking in their sides, but if someone says, "Well, get up and move," they say, "No, it's okay." They're not in enough pain to make a change.

About 20 years ago, I was at a seminar and the speaker stated that there are only two real motivators in life: Pleasure and Pain, and I agree. We strive to acquire pleasure or avoid pain. We work hard to afford holidays, have fun, acquire our little chattels and toys, or perhaps do good deeds, all of which give us pleasure. We work equally hard to avoid painful situations: paying the bills so we don't have the electricity cut off, paying the mortgage so the bank doesn't repossess the house, and so on. But the fact is, pain is a greater motivator than pleasure. It's proven.

A simple example: let's say one of your short-term goals is to have a tropical island holiday and you have worked out that it's going to cost you $5,000. Your friends have done a deal with a travel agent and if you book within the month you can get the same holiday for just $3,000! But as much as you would love to book, you only have $500 in your holiday account. Your friends say, "Don't worry, we'll send you a postcard."

The following day, you get a sign that you are a very important person in the form of a personalised, registered letter from the Commissioner of Taxation! In the letter, the commissioner states that their records indicate you have overlooked paying the correct amount of income tax for the past three years. If you do not pay $5,000 within seven days, you will be incarcerated and given three months' free accommodation and food, courtesy of the government! How fast do you think it would take you to find $5,000 under those circumstances? One way or another, you would find it in a heartbeat, right?

I did have one creative audience member suggest that another option would be to get the money, go to the tropics and not return.

I love lateral thinkers. But the point is that we will run away from a root canal faster than we will run towards a piece of chocolate cake. We fear pain more than we desire pleasure. Science proves this: research into investing by two American psychologists showed that the desire to avoid a financial loss is twice as strong as the pleasure we get from a financial gain. From finding the money to pay a delinquent tax bill and avoid going to jail, to losing weight and getting fit to avoid having a second heart attack, we find heroic levels of motivation when we try to avoid unpleasant or frightening consequences. You can use this as leverage in your quest to motivate change!

Fast forward five or 10 years into the future and see the life you think you'll be living. Now visualise the life you would *like* to be living. Finding your true dissatisfaction level is all about seeing what is blocking you or causing you pain and why. We have a difficult time admitting that we're unhappy with our lives. We don't want to admit that we've made poor choices. We fear alienating the people in our lives by insisting on change. However, seeing your true level of dissatisfaction — and admitting to it honestly and openly — is what gives you the power to identify your gap and start doing something about it. So quit worrying about what other people will think and start asking questions:

TRUE LEVEL OF DISSATISFACTION WORKSHEET

1. What is the central pain in my life or career that I've been avoiding or denying?

_____

_____

2. What have I been doing to paint or wallpaper over that pain so I don't have to confront it, and why?

_____

_____

3. What wants and needs eat at me every day, aching to be satisfied?

_____

_____

4. If I could create a life that would satisfy my chief want and need, what would that life look like? How would it differ from my life today?

_____

_____

5. Is this the best I can do, or am I capable of more?

_____

_____

Keep in mind that when I talk about needs, I'm not talking about the needs psychologist Abraham Maslow so neatly defined — food, shelter, sex, social connection. These are primary human needs. They are important and you have to satisfy them; until you do, you can't move on to the realisation phase. You'll be building a house on a bad foundation. But you can reverse engineer those basic needs. This is about project managing the outcome of your life and designing a journey that feeds your hunger for independence, creativity, making a difference in the world, controlling your time – whatever you need to feel complete.

Need is about becoming a different person. Your gap is the distance between who you are today and who you could become. Everything else is process.

Need is about becoming a different person. Your gap is the distance between who you are today and who you could become. Everything else is process. That means that change is *achievable*. Once you identify the problem, you're halfway to solving it. Once you go through this process, describe your gap below as a "Where I am/Where I want to be" statement:

MY GAP

Where am I now in my finances, career and relationship?_____

What's my greatest satisfaction? _____

What's my greatest dissatisfaction?_____

Where do I want my finances, career and relationships to be in five years?

_____

_____

In 10 years?_____

_____

_____

Bridging Your Gap

American financial titan J.P. Morgan said, "The wise man bridges the gap by laying out the path by means of which he can get from where he is to where he wants to go." Once you have identified the gap in your life and career, you need to create a plan to build a bridge across that chasm. I'm not talking about some rickety rope-and-sticks project; this needs to be sturdy enough to withstand the storms and reversals that any journey to a new life will encounter. Because:

> *Bridging your gap will take time.*

Just as important is this truth:

> *Every huge bridge is made up of hundreds of smaller spans.*

All good outcomes take time. I didn't go from a being a trolley boy to achieving the lifestyle I now enjoy overnight. It took years to figure out what I wanted from my life and build my consulting and speaking brand. During that time, I have flown through some turbulent skies (including several typhoons), avoided a few disasters and had a couple of emergency landings, but that's just life, and I live to tell the tale. All in all, it's been a fantastic journey. Take control and make yours a great one, too.

I'd like to share with you some of the principles I used to bridge my gap. I wish someone had shared them with me earlier in my life:

- *Knowledge is your most important tool.* Acknowledge you have a gap and acquire the knowledge you need to bridge the gap. Figure out your "how, what and why"; learn how to change, how to improve and how to stay motivated. It's all well and good to aspire to transition from a marketing executive to a restorer of vintage cars, but you'd better know something about autos and the vintage car business first. Do your research. Associate with like-minded, positive people. Join clubs or business groups. Find a mentor who's doing what you want to do. Ask questions.

- *Don't focus on material outcomes.* Yes, you want to make a good living when you finally make it across your gap. Of course you do; your income is the fuel for your lifestyle. But crossing your gap is about becoming your best self, not acquiring more stuff. Remember the adaptation principle? The one outcome that no one can take away — the one that never loses its value — is becoming a stronger, wiser, happier, more fully realised human being. Don't get sucked into the myth that a bigger house or nicer car will change your life. Often, it's the exact opposite: shedding material possessions, de-cluttering, simplifying and downsizing can be the ultimate liberation for some.

> *Don't get sucked into the myth that a bigger house or nicer car will change your life.*

- *Be realistic.* Not all the dreams people have when they hit a transition point in life are achievable. It's like New Year's resolutions. At 11.55pm on New Year's Eve, someone who is lubricated with copious quantities of bourbon stands up and proclaims to everyone within earshot: "This is my last cigarette ever!" Or there's the infamous, "I'm going to go to the gym every morning before work, lose 10 kilos in a month and get a body like Arnold Schwarzenegger in his prime!" Hic. You know the type, right? The thing is, our subconscious mind knows we're not going to do what we promise, and it discards our good intentions as a combination of cheap bourbon and dissatisfaction with life.

> The thing is, our subconscious mind knows we're not going to do what we promise, and it discards our good intentions as a combination of cheap bourbon and dissatisfaction with life.

I'm a realistic optimist. Most things are possible but not necessarily probable. It's possible that one day we may be able to fly to Mars, but it's not probable that we will get there in the next 10 or 20 years. So be careful not to set yourself unrealistic goals, as it will only lead to frustration and failure. Starting a business? Very possible and probable. Losing 35 kilograms and completing an Ironman? Possible, with a lot of work making it probable. Buying a sailboat and spending 10 years cruising the Seychelles and Maldives? Possible and probable, with the right planning.

My simple rule is this: if your goal requires an insane amount of luck, defies the laws of physics or physiology, or demands so much of your time that everyone in your life will hate you, forget it. Otherwise, as long as you know the work and effort you have ahead of you, go for it no matter how crazy everyone says or thinks you are. Prove them wrong!

- *Break it down into milestones*, or your waypoints on your flight path. You know the saying, "A journey begins with a single step." Crossing your gap can only happen one step at a time, and the more radical the change, the more specific those steps need to be. Breaking your journey into stages and steps — with achievable milestones along the way — is a sound strategy not just for managing your time and efforts, but also for keeping the whole enterprise from becoming overwhelming.

What do you need to do today? What do you need to do next month and next year? Where should you be in 18 months? I suggest creating your flight plan and literally mapping out your journey. Be specific about what you need to do — take a critical university course, book a holiday, obtain bank finance, forge a key business relationship — and write them along a timeline. At intervals, set milestones you can aim for, whether that means losing 25 kilos or passing the test for your financial planner's license. After all, only foolish and short-term Pilots would ever head off into the wild blue yonder without a flight plan, right?

Also, get in touch with your inner Buddhist. Say what? Well, in Buddhism there's a principle that says you shouldn't focus on the outcome of a plan because you can't manifest the final result. In other words, you can't say, "I'm going to save five thousand dollars," and have the money appear on your desk. What you *can* do is focus on taking the right actions that should result in the desired outcome. If you're trying to put away a lot of money, that might include limiting your spending, taking a second job and so on. By ignoring the outcome and taking steady, disciplined actions, you become the kind of person who can create the results you want.

- *Give yourself a deadline.* What's your finish line? When do you want to take those final steps across that bridge and have the life and career to which you aspire? Six months? Two years? Ten years? Whatever your timeline, set it and adhere to it. Remember, we only have so much time in this world. Use yours wisely.

Writing a Letter to Your Friend

Let's take a step back from all of this for a second. I'm well aware that thinking about turning your back on your current career or way of life can induce a bit of vertigo. From the vantage point of your current life, the future you dream of can seem as far away as the moon, and attaining that future can seem as impossible as flying there by flapping your arms.

When I conduct goal-setting courses, one of my exercises involves asking my audience members to write a letter to their best friend. I say, "Imagine if today you lost all contact with your best friend. You know they are okay, but they seem to have vanished. Now fast forward five years. I come along and say, 'Great news! Here's your friend's email address – they've been in the police protection program (that's the sort of friends you have)!' You are delighted, and start writing them an email."

But remember, it's five years into the future. What will you be writing? Where are you living, what's your house like, what cars are you driving, what holidays have you had, how are you doing? How proud are you of the picture you're painting for your friend? Is your friend going to be impressed or are they going to think, "Gee, Bob hasn't come very far since our days at the office. What on Earth has the man been doing with his time?"

If you think it's the latter, then write two letters. First, write a letter that reflects your life today. Then write the letter you'd love to write to your best friend, describing your life of travel, prosperity, status and independence. It's your job to turn the second letter into a reality.

How Much is Your Dream Going to Cost?

As you work towards that, however, there's one other factor to consider: the cost of your dream. As you start researching and planning, you'll start finding out what it will cost to make the changes you have in mind. Every dream costs, and cost is not just about money. It's also about accepting that things will change, and there may be some emotional cost.

Every dream costs, and cost is not just about money. It's also about accepting that things will change, and there may be some emotional cost.

The question is whether achieving your dream is worth the cost. For example, if your dream is to become a prize-winning author but doing so means abandoning your spouse and children so you can write, the dream is probably not worth the cost. Possible costs include:

- *Money.* This is the obvious one. If you want to go back to school, open a restaurant or buy a yacht, you're going to spend. If you want to retire early, you're going to need to save.

- *Sacrifice.* Your flight to your goals will require some trade-offs. You may have to sacrifice some things now to have other things later. Saving money is a classic example. If you want to save money for your dream home, you can't waste all your weekly income on things that aren't important .

- *Change.* A great saying goes, "If nothing changes, nothing changes." Change for some can be traumatic, which is why the most stressful events in our lives — death, divorce, job loss, relocating — all involve sudden, wrenching change. We get comfortable with being comfortable. But leaping across your gap may mean leaving some parts of your current life behind, and that's difficult and frightening. It may also create waves.

Friends, family and colleagues might feel rejected, confused or angry. However, the people in your life who truly want the best for you will adapt as you change and will still be there for you.

- *Delayed gratification.* If you're determined to launch your own retail store, you'll have to give up on expensive tropical holidays for a while. If your dream is to get in shape and run a marathon, say goodbye to burgers and pizza. You will almost certainly have to give up some of what you enjoy in the short term in order to get what you want in the long term.

- *Work.* Building a bridge across your gap will take more work than you've ever done in your life. Perhaps going back to school and attaining your advanced degree. Learning a new skill. Getting up at four in the morning to run. Name the dream and there's a long list of back-breaking tasks associated with being good at it. The encouraging news is that while it's giving you a new life, the work will also mould you into a new and better person.

- *Time.* We buy our dreams with time. No other currency is accepted. Depending on your dream, you may have to sacrifice time away from home, children and family to do what you want to do. Once you figure out how much time is needed, you can decide how much of your limited supply you're willing to spend.

Goodbye to the "Misery Guts"

There's excess luggage, anchors, and drag nets in your life. Trust me, everyone has them. To find them, try this eye-opener: write the names of the four or five people you communicate with most often in your life today — family, friends and co-workers. Now draw one big circle around those names and have a really good look at the people in that circle. You're looking at your life! Now, before you start rejecting that statement, let me explain. Would you agree that the people in that circle influence what you talk about, what restaurants you visit, what movies you see and more? The people in your circle determine whether you are talking about football or investment properties and shares. They influence you and you influence them. Right? That's your "circle of influence".

The people in your circle should be enthusiastic, energetic, autonomous and focused...

Now, I want you to realise that there's only one constant in your circle, and that's you. The others will come and go. The circle you have today is most likely different from the circle you had 10 or 15 years ago, right? It will change again over time, but be mindful of who you allow into your circle. Here's why: there are two types of people you need to be aware of in your circle. Hopefully, you have plenty of the first. These are the people with as much energy and enthusiasm about something as you have! They are people with whom you exchange positive energy, enjoy talking to and walk away from feeling uplifted. If there isn't someone like that in your circle now, don't worry – you can be in more than one circle at any given time. Join a club or an association. Catch up with some like-minded, positive people once or twice a month, such as a speaking group, fishing club or mothers' group. Exchange positive energy. Find people who inspire, re-energise and encourage you.

The second type of person you need to be aware of is the type I affectionately refer to as the "misery guts." They're also known as "fun sponges" or "black holes of energy". You know the type – they complain about everything. "It's too hot. It's too cold. You can't please them if you tried." If they won the lottery but had to share $10 million with someone else, they would be crying all night! They can always find something to complain about.

Now, you can still love and hug a misery guts – they may be family – but whatever you do, don't let them suck the energy out of you. Keep them at a safe distance!

You see, successful people are relatively independent, but a misery guts needs company and they are typically great recruiters. For example, you've probably experienced this scenario: you just come out of a training session at work and the misery guts is hanging around the coffee machine, waiting to recruit. "Hey, Joe, what do you think? This is all crap. It will never work, eh?" Now, Joe doesn't want to argue, so the easiest thing for Joe to say is, "Yeah," and the misery guts has hooked one! "Hey, Mary. Joe and I were just saying..." sound familiar? On to the next. They need to hold people back because, God forbid should you do well and achieve success, you'll make them look bad! But they're too lazy to strive for their goals; it's easier to maintain a level of mediocrity and bring others down to their level. Sound familiar? Misery guts are Passengers for life; in fact, they don't even want the plane to take off. They don't want others to succeed because it will make them look bad. If you know such people, cut them out of your life if you can.

Sometimes, a misery guts will be a family member or other person you can't physically remove from your circle. In that case, be aware of their negative energy and don't let it affect you. You can still love and hug them, but don't let them get in the way of what you want to do and who you want to be.

Your goal is to create a positive "circle of influence": a tight-knit family of three, four or perhaps 10 people with

The people in your circle should be enthusiastic, energetic, autonomous and focused — people who will exchange positive energy, critique your ideas, share their wisdom, encourage and bring out the best in you.

whom you spend most of your time communicating. The people in your circle should be enthusiastic, energetic, autonomous and focused — people who will exchange positive energy, critique your ideas, share their wisdom, encourage and bring out the best in you. These are some of the key traits to look for:

- Optimism
- Energy
- Enthusiasm
- Resilience
- People skills
- Empathy
- Presence
- Honesty
- Focus
- Compassion
- Discipline

Are You Circle Worthy?

Consider this. If you are part of a positive circle of influence, you're not allowed to simply take from other people. You must give as well. Are you the kind of person others would want in their circle? Are you circle worthy? That's one of the big questions I pose to you: if your friends were doing the "circle of influence" exercise and were looking at your name, what would they be thinking about you? How would your friends and peers rate you on the traits in the above list? That's important, because the qualities that would make you a great addition to someone's positive circle of influence will help you bridge your gap. My advice? Rate yourself on a 1-10 scale on each of those traits and work on the ones where you don't measure up to your own standards. Better yet, ask friends to rate you – if you dare. Then see where you can improve. You'll be a better person, Pilot and member of people's circle.

Key Questions

- What keeps me up at night?
- Is my dream realistic? If not, why not?
- How can I change my dream to make it attainable?
- Who should I consider removing from my circle of influence?
- What do I need to sacrifice in order to have the life I want?
- How much time is my dream likely to cost? Is that cost worth paying, or can I reduce it?
- What qualities make me circle worthy?
- What qualities need work?

The Million-Dollar Question

Who do I know who has already bridged this gap and how can that person be a role model for my journey?

Always Start With the End in Mind

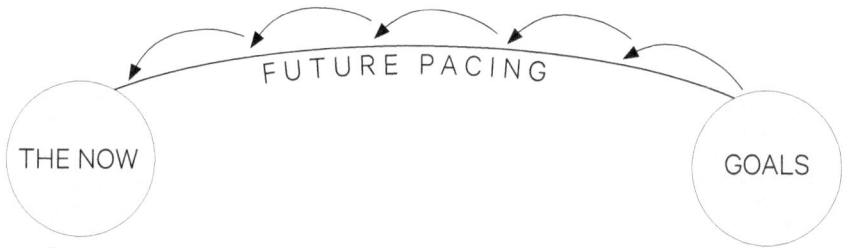

FUTURE PACING

THE NOW

GOALS

Revise engineer your goals and dreams,
and set your way points

*"The path to our destination is not always a straight
one. We go down the wrong road, we get lost, we
turn back. Maybe it doesn't matter which road we
embark on. Maybe what matters is that we embark."*

Barbara Hall

Things creep up on us. That's a fact of life. It's why we can go from being fit and trim when we're 30 years old to waking up when we're 50 and finding a cubby face staring back from the mirror. How can such a thing happen? It happens three grams at a time. Three tiny grams of fat every day, for 365 days, is a kilogram. Ten years later: bingo! We're 10 kilos heavier. It happens slowly, over time, because we let things go. We lose our focus. We get complacent. We lose the urgency of staying fit, saving money, working on our marriage or pursuing the goals on life's bucket list. We get comfortable!

> *Things creep up on us. That's a fact of life. It's why we can go from being fit and trim when we're 30 years old to waking up when we're 50 and finding a chubby face staring back from the mirror.*

People always say: "Life is short." But that's relative; 80 years is a long time. Life only *appears* short when you look back at what you didn't accomplish because you didn't maintain that sense of urgency. Imagine this scenario: instead of gaining a kilogram a year for 20 years, you wake up tomorrow morning 20 kilos heavier than you had been when you went to bed. That would be an "Oh my God!" moment, wouldn't it? You would be terrified for your health and future, and you'd be shocked into action.

That's what happens to us in slow motion when we put things off until later, pass opportunities, veer off course or defer an important choice until a later time because it makes us uncomfortable. We lose ground that we may never get back. The truth is that nothing happens overnight. Success in career, health, life and relationships is a matter of small changes and smart choices made consistently and determinedly over years.

Take former Australian Rules football player Rex Hunt. After a career as a police officer and a teacher, Rex went on to become a first-grade football player. It wasn't until he'd been doing regular fishing reports on the radio for more than 10 years that he finally "hit it big" and got a long-running and successful television program called **Rex Hunt Fishing Adventures**. One day, I was fishing with his son, Matthew, and talking about Rex's career. Matthew said, "People think Dad just popped up out of nowhere. But it's taken him 20 years to become an overnight success."

That's an incredibly common theme, in sports, television, movies, publishing, music, business etc. We don't see the years and years of hard work, mistakes and disasters that lead to the big breakthroughs. We only see the breakthroughs and assume they came out of the blue. But it's delusional to believe in overnight success. Getting what you want instantly is usually a disaster.

A shocking percentage of lottery winners wind up bankrupt, divorced or die at their own hand. Why? Because they continue to have the same bad habits they had before they hit the jackpot. For the vast majority of us, even if we got incredibly lucky and experienced inhumanly fast success, we would still be the same people we were before it happened. Even if you won $100 million tomorrow, you would still have the same bad habits, the same poor discipline or the same lack of confidence. If you think like a poor person, you'll find a way to make yourself poor. Your mind will take you where you let it, but that's another chapter.

The reason some people enjoy sustained success for decades is because the journey to that success changes them.

The reason some people enjoy sustained success for decades is because the journey to that success changes them. The only way they can finish their great novel or get that internet company off the ground is by learning to be disciplined, optimistic, persevering and frugal. The process of making change gradually transforms you into someone who can sustain the change. It's like becoming a black belt in martial arts. When you start, you just want to learn to be like Bruce Lee. But as you progress through years of training and testing, it's not only your skill at punching and kicking that develops. It's also your humility, restraint and confidence. By the time you earn your black belt, you've become someone who doesn't need to fight. The journey has changed you.

Destiny = Goal + Time + Effort

I often hear people talk about something being their "destiny". Really? Convincing yourself that everything is pre-determined and that your fate has already been mapped out for you is a disempowering mindset. In my experience, describing something as your destiny is a subtle way of saying, "I don't have to plan or do any work because it's going to happen for me in time." That's nonsense.

Planning for a specific outcome at a specific time in your future is the difference between being a Pilot and a Passenger.

Destiny is nothing more than a goal attached to a timeframe, as in: "In five years, I will own my own charter sailboat business." But it's not enough to simply say it and wish for it. Don't just say, "I want to be in a new career." Be specific. Planning for a specific outcome at a specific time in your future is the difference between being a Pilot and a Passenger. In short, we have our next Raw Fact:

To get where you want to go, always plan with the end in mind.

Those who enjoy extraordinary success take action to reverse engineer their lives, looking at where they want to be at a certain point in the future and working backwards from there.

This takes dedicated thought and planning. It's much easier, of course, to go with the flow, be fatalistic and accept what comes as what is meant to be. But that's the path to mediocrity, and you're not here for that. You are reading this book because you know there is so much more you want to and can achieve. Greatness doesn't come from accepting the way things are. If Steve Jobs had accepted the way things were, he might never have launched Apple. Sir Richard Branson might never have built his Virgin empire. The fact is, if you keep doing what you have been doing, you'll keep getting what you've been getting.

Greatness doesn't come from accepting the way things are. If Steve Jobs had accepted the way things were, he might never have launched Apple.

Remember, there are always options and opportunities, and you have the power of choice. Keep your eyes on the prize and don't forget to enjoy the flight and celebrate when you reach milestones.

Active versus Passive Living

One of the first steps I counsel my audiences to take is to live *actively* instead of *passively*. Passive living means accepting things the way they are and presuming that we as individuals have little power to change our path. It's disempowering; an act of surrender to the forces sweeping us towards whatever we end up doing.

Of course, we're all headed to the same place: over that roaring waterfall of mortality to whatever waits beyond. But along the way, we have infinite power to shape our journey – *if we choose to exercise it*. The first step is to choose to live with what I call *healthy urgency*. This should be the motivating factor in your life; it's the *need* to make things happen that puts you in the Pilot's seat, not an ordinary Passenger's seat on a budget airline flight.

This means living with *presence and mindfulness*, being fully aware of the choices you make and the choices you refuse to make and how they impact what happens to you. Think of it as being a gymnast or tightrope walker. If you're walking a tightrope between two tall buildings, you have no choice but to be 100 per cent present in the moment. If you're not, you will soon be snapped back into the present – if only for the last few seconds of your life. You are keenly aware of how your muscles are moving, what the wind is doing, how your weight is shifting and how far along the rope you are.

Active living means having the same awareness of how everything you do —your self-talk, circle of friends and your approach with friends, clients, customers and more — shapes your future.

Active living means having the same awareness of how everything you do —your self-talk, circle of friends and your approach with friends, clients, customers and more — shapes your future. You've probably heard of the concept called the "butterfly effect", in which a small change in a complex system — such as a butterfly flapping its wings — can lead to a massive change in that system. You are constantly having a butterfly effect on your own life. It's exciting and empowering. It makes sense to be conscious of how your actions and choices shape your future, and to consciously change those actions and choices to create the future you want.

There are people who feel they are happier living passively, unconsciously. Some fear failure. They give themselves excuses not to try so they don't have to risk falling down. They often have poor self-esteem and are terrified of the regret they think they will feel if they stumble. However, here's a truth to remember:

We regret the things we don't do far more than the things we do.

In other words, don't be afraid to try something: new goals, new career or a new hobby. Don't let fear or complacency hold you back. And don't let failure get in the way of your success. View failures as merely air pockets en route to your destination.

The acronym for FEAR is: False Evidence Appearing Real, and fear will cripple you.

The acronym for FEAR is: False Emotions Appearing Real, and fear will cripple you.

Knowledge Dispels Fear

The great irony is that the fear of failure makes many people define themselves as victims. But that fear just holds you back and regret is waiting at the end of the path. If you try something and make a fool of yourself, at least you can take pride in having the courage to have a go – and now you can try again! As Shakespeare wrote: "Cowards die a thousand times before their deaths." No one wants to lie awake at night, thinking: "If only..." And, of course, if you fail, you get to try again.

We have all heard of the saying: "Never put off until tomorrow what you can do today." Well, I reckon I've worked it out. You see, if you do it today and you like it, you can do it again tomorrow!

The other group that tends to prefer to live passively is the people who can't handle uncertainty. Deep down, they don't believe in their own *self-efficacy*, the belief that they can handle whatever comes along. They always have excuses why other people have achieved what they always wanted to achieve: the other person is luckier, they got the better breaks, and so on. Or others may start off full of motivation and vigour, but still harbour a fear of uncertainty. Eventually, their desire fades and they revert to their old ways. The pain of changing remains greater than the pain of staying where they are, so they stay.

Optimists believe that a failure in one area does not make them failures in other areas. Pessimists tend to believe that a failure in one area means they are failures at everything.

Change Your Self-Talk

In 1990, psychologist Martin Seligman published a brilliant concept that in many ways established the field of positive psychology: *learned optimism*. People can learn, he said, to see adversity in a way that trains them to be optimistic and empowered about their circumstances. Bad things still happen, but learned optimists see the reasons behind those bad events differently to pessimists, who are steeped in what Seligman named *learned helplessness*:

- *Permanence*: Optimists believe negative events are the result of temporary problems that can be dealt with. Pessimists believe bad outcomes are caused by permanent factors that are unlikely to change.

- *Pervasiveness*: Optimists believe that a failure in one area does not make them failures in other areas. Pessimists tend to believe that a failure in one area means they are failures at everything.

- *Personalisation*: Optimists recognise that some failures occur due to circumstances totally out of their control. Pessimists believe they failed because they weren't good enough, even if what happened was out of their hands.

I bring this up because whether you've learned to be an optimist or pessimist will have a profound effect on your self-talk, which will shape your future. People who are optimistic tend to believe they can bounce back from setbacks; pessimists tend to feel helpless in the grip of causes larger than themselves, and so they are prone to give up easily. Self-talk becomes self-belief. Your beliefs will shape your thinking and your thoughts will become your actions. If you continually tell yourself that you can't achieve your dream because you're not smart enough or rich enough, then you're right. You will find a way to sabotage yourself or never get started at all. On the other hand, if you develop a habit of finding empowering explanations for what happens and make your self-talk positive, you are more likely to try the audacious things that change lives for the better.

One tactic that works very well: *fake it till you make it*. Life is a lot like theatre; there will be days when you don't feel like performing or smiling, when your positive thinking goes out the window. On such days, you need to fake it in order to make it happen, and every day is show time. Force yourself to smile and be positive, and you will be surprised at how effectively your brain will translate this into your behaviour.

> Life is a lot like theatre; there will be days when you don't feel like performing or smiling, when your positive thinking goes out the window.

Another effective way to change your habitual way of thinking is to find a role model. Emulate someone who has done or achieved what you want to do or achieve, and model them. What makes them tick and what can you learn from them? Learn how to look as though you're a confident player in your field and you'll start to think like one. You might even fool yourself into changing your mental habits. That will change who you are and who you can become.

Future Pacing

I first came across this concept in Stephen Covey's book *The 7 Habits of Highly Effective People*. Another terrific technique is what I call "future pacing". Know precisely what you want to achieve during a given timeframe. Your timeframe could be short (a one-hour sales call), long (retire in 10 years), or in between. Whatever it is, you're not waiting for things to happen. You're taking conscious action to manifest outcomes.

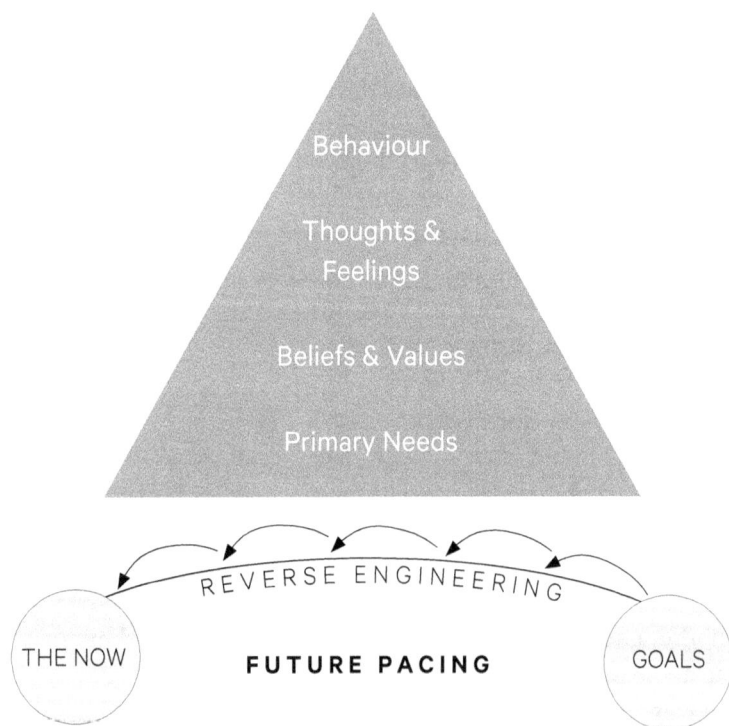

Behaviour

Thoughts & Feelings

Beliefs & Values

Primary Needs

REVERSE ENGINEERING

THE NOW   **FUTURE PACING**   GOALS

Future pacing is a type of reverse engineering. Imagine that you're planning a magnificent holiday 12 months from today. You've made the commitment and you have set the date. Yahoo! The first thing you would most likely do is go on the internet and research your options: flights, accommodation, activities, requirements and so on. Eventually, you settle on an airline, hotel, car hire and activities. It's all very exciting, and you have worked out what your holiday is going to cost. There are also all the other things you need to do to make this dream holiday a reality: apply for your passport and visa, book the flights, book accommodation, get vaccinations, get time off work, etc.

Now, let's say that your dream holiday is going to cost $5,000, but you only have $100 in your holiday fund. You're going to need to save about $400 per month. You set a budget and make a savings plan. You start taking your lunch to work. You sell the spare fridge that's been in the garage for years. You start cooking at home five nights a week instead of eating out every night. As your savings grow, so does the smile on your face. These are small trade-offs when you keep your eye on the prize. Your money is growing and you're ticking off your "must-do" items and everything is in place. Congratulations — you're on your way to a great holiday!

You've just future paced. You've tied a particular outcome to a timeframe and identified what you must do to achieve it. And you've followed through. But let's say it's now 11 months down the track and you haven't applied for your passport or visa. You have been telling yourself for 11 months that you'll do it tomorrow, but you haven't booked your flight or accommodation (which is now no longer on special) because you thought a better deal might come up. Also, your savings plan hasn't gone particularly well. What are your chances of setting off on your holiday in four weeks' time? Zero!

Future pacing is all about planning the work and working the plan. If you don't work the plan, there's every chance that in 11 months' time, you'll be no closer to having your dream holiday. You'll be forced into taking desperate measures or giving up on your cherished goal.

Areas where you can use future pacing to lay out career goals include:

- Starting a business
- Planning for early retirement
- Aiming for a promotion
- Pursuing an advanced degree

But don't be limited by that list. You can also apply this strategy to your life plan, holidays, fitness goals (such as running a triathlon) or personal finance goals (such as paying off debts). If you can identify a discrete span of time and set an objective to be achieved in that time, you can future pace.

It's all about keeping your eye on the prize.

Your Bucket List

Of course, follow-through can be tricky. It's one thing to make plans and grand pronouncements, and quite another to show the discipline, day after day, to keep plugging money into your holiday account or racking up the miles in your lonely marathon-training routine. That's why so many people fail in their quest to bring about real change: they don't account for the need to engage their emotions.

In recent years — and thanks, in part, to a hit US film starring Jack Nicholson and Morgan Freeman —more people have become aware of the power of the "bucket list" for engaging emotions. A bucket list is simply a list of things you want to do before you "kick the bucket", a uniquely American idiom that means to "cark it", "push up daisies", or "shuffle off this mortal coil". Plenty of people I know have started putting their lists together, saying, in effect, that life is short and there's much to accomplish.

The bucket list is an example of a powerful tool called *forced urgency*. Accidental urgency is when circumstances force you into emergency mode: you have to take radical action now or bad outcomes will result. Surviving a heart attack is an example of an event creating a sense of accidental urgency; afraid for your life, you're likely to embark on a profound change in diet, exercise and lifestyle.

In talking about creating forced urgency, I'm not suggesting you put yourself under so much pressure that you become obsessive. A healthy level of urgency helps us focus and motivates us through a positive journey to an enjoyable destination. Forced urgency doesn't wait for circumstances to put you into emergency mode. It means seeking out reasons to feel that you have no choice but to take radical action *now*. It's the act of consciously pursuing the "I need to do something!" impulse rather than waiting for it to strike. You can't wait for urgency to find you. What if it takes 20 years?

A healthy level of urgency helps us focus and motivates us through a positive journey to an enjoyable destination. Forced urgency doesn't wait for circumstances to put you into emergency mode.

You create forced urgency with a (healthy) *forced crisis*. You put yourself in situations where you will receive either strong negative ("God, I can't have this in my life!") or strong positive ("God, if I don't have this in my life, I'll die!") stimulus. You get out of your comfort zone: shadow a job, go on a trip, get on a scale. More often than not, negative feelings — fear, embarrassment, regret — will motivate you and create urgency, but the pain you're in becomes your friend. It keeps you focused and on task, moving forward towards your goal.

The alternative is that the world around you eventually changes and you get left behind. If you don't act, someone will act for you, and maybe not at the best time. And you'll find yourself lamenting, "I wish I had done this years ago." Unfortunately, you don't get that time back! Be the Pilot, not the Passenger. If you hate your job, don't wait to be fired – fire yourself and create change.

Know Your 'Why'

Starting at the end requires that you understand why you want what you want. Why does your goal excite and animate you? What kind of life do you envisage yourself having? Why do you do what you do today? Are you on course or do you crave a change?

The greatest power source comes from your own internal motivation, your positive mindset. It's easy to veer off course, after all. Remember, most people will take the path of least resistance – will you?

Change is hard for most people. It can be hard, frightening and time-consuming drudgery. You need a power source of positive energy to keep you motivated and on the straight and narrow path. The greatest power source comes from your own internal motivation, your positive mindset. It's easy to veer off course, after all. Remember, most people will take the path of least resistance – will you?

Why do you do what you do? Certainly, money plays a role, but the journey of life has to be important for its own sake. Money matters, but money doesn't inspire. The enjoyment of the journey is what makes us smile and keeps us going. We all like to have "good days" when we come home from work feeling good, pat the dog, cuddle the kids and relax with a feeling contentment and accomplishment. They certainly beat the days of stress, anger and road rage! You finally get home, get out of the car and kick the dog (and it's not even your dog), grumble at your partner and kids ... and set the scene for round two!

Have you ever stopped to think about what elements constitute a good day for you? I often get clients to write the attributes that make up a "good day" for them: satisfied customers, no complaints, closed deals, getting on with colleagues, having a few laughs, no traffic stress, and so on. Notice how few of these have anything to do with money? Those are the things that keep us going. Then I ask my clients to write the elements that constitutes a "bad day": customer complaints, losing a sale, missing deadlines, gossip, not getting along with colleagues, running late, getting caught in peak-hour traffic, dealing with negative people, and so on.

Write your own lists, good and bad. Then, identify which factors are controllable and which are beyond your control? You see, we spend so much mental energy and time worrying about things we can't control that we sometimes forget to control the things we *can* control; the very things you can control that bring

*We spend so much mental energy and time worrying about things we can't control that we sometimes forget to control the things we **can** control; the things you can control that bring you pleasure and make your days more positive, productive and enjoyable.*

you pleasure and make your days more positive, productive and enjoyable.

Here's an example of wasting energy on things beyond your control. During the global financial crisis, I attended a conference and there were about 50 delegates milling around in the foyer having coffee. A man stood amongst a small group of people, almost crying over the crash of the stock market. He held his brow in his hand, moaning, "It's dropped so much, God it's crashed so much ..." and on he went. The other men and I listened sympathetically, thinking he must have lost everything and was borderline suicidal. I asked him, "Harry, what shares did you have?" He looked at me with surprise and said, "Oh, I don't have any shares, it's just what the papers and the news are saying!"

We all looked at each other and rolled our eyes, and the other men walked away. I simply and calmly said, "Harry, you're an idiot. You have totally disempowered yourself. You are allowing the misery guts within the media to poison your mind with things that you can't control and that have no direct bearing on you." It was a big wake-up call for him.

Be aware of what you can't control but
focus on what you can control.

You can't control the weather, but you can fly around the storm!

As you start to reverse engineer your outcome, figure out what matters most to you and what's in your control. If you have a strong emotional stake — again, urgency — in the result of your planning, you're more apt to proceed smartly and not look back. If there are negative elements in your life that are out of your control, find a way to change them. Stop smoking. If fuel prices go up and cause you pain, either accept it or do something about it: buy a vehicle that uses less fuel, buy a bike, catch a train or earn more money. It's all about choice and priorities, but don't simply whine about it.

There's an old saying: "If you're not part of the solution, you're part of the problem." You can apply this same rationale to your attitude. When it comes to the things you can't control, it's best to respond with calm and wisdom. The key is to **respond**, not **react**. Responding means thinking about your next action; reacting is merely acting on reflex without considering the consequences. When something happens, you need to calmly revise your flight plan and keep going.

There's an old saying: "If you're not part of the solution, you're part of the problem." You can apply this same rationale to your attitude.

Be careful about playing the devil's advocate too much, though. It can turn your mind exclusively towards the gloomy and negative. It's easy to become a misery guts. Be a realistic optimist!

Make Your Plan

Yeah, all right, Alex. All this cheerleading and positive self-talk business is fine, but what about the plan to start at the end and work backwards? We're there, so let's talk about that. Armed with your healthy sense of urgency and your positive "why", you should be able to look ahead in time and see where you want to be after you've bridged your gap. Knowing specifically what you want — and naming it precisely — is critical to success.

Most people shoot first and whatever they hit they call the target. This is like an overly enthusiastic person getting their pilot's license, so keen to fly that they hops in the plane and takes off, then runs out of fuel and rather than ditching in the ocean makes an emergency landing on an uncharted island infested with venomous snakes and inhabited by hungry cannibals. After being rescued, someone asks, "Why did you land there?" Embarrassed, they answer, "Uh, what do you mean? I meant to land there all along." Yeah, right, sure you did.

Rash action rarely leads to satisfying results. Too many people take the "ready, fire, aim!" approach to their future. Eager and jittery about taking some kind — *any* kind — of action, they go in the wrong direction, spending energy and time without any sort of target. Then they hit something and even if it's not what they want, they call it the target to avoid embarrassment, never try again and slink back to the Passenger seat.

Having a plan is like setting a flight path. It dramatically increases your odds of arriving at your chosen destination.

Having a plan is like setting a flight path. It dramatically increases your odds of arriving at your chosen destination. When building your plan, here are the steps I suggest you follow:

- **Keep your eye on the prize.** Look at the end, your goal for this leg of your journey. What do you want your career, business and life to look like in a certain timeframe? Be detailed about your income, occupation, leisure time, where you'll live and even what kind of car you'll drive.

- **Figure out what it's going to take to get to that destination.** What are the critical milestones en route? Prioritise them and account for time. Do you need to acquire new skills or knowledge? To associate with different people? To get up early and work out? To raise money for a new company? Step backwards from your goal and take the world apart piece by piece. What are you missing right now that you need to have?

- **Figure out the resources you'll need.** Money, contacts, technology — have a brain dump and list them all. You'll need to find a way to get them.

- **You'll also need allies.** Who can you share (and perhaps include) your dream and enthusiasm with? Who will understand and encourage you? Who will be happy to see you succeed? Who can you count on to help, mentor and encourage you as you go through this process? On the other hand, what people in your life will be sources of negativity? Remove them from your circle or change circles. You'll want to avoid them as much as possible to keep them from poisoning your positive energy.

- **Make your calendar.** You can do this on a computer or even on a wall chart, as long as you use the calendar to track your progress and motivate you. The calendar is your "flight plan" that shows your milestones — your actions and goals attached to specific timeframes; for example, "$50,000 in start-up funding raised by July 1". Your calendar becomes your bible, your guiding document.

- **Finally, create an accountability structure.** How will you ensure that you don't slacken and veer off your path? You could engage a mentor or coach. Give certain people permission to hold you responsible and demand progress of you. Will you set up rewards you can only claim if you reach certain goals? Remember, "If it is to be, it's up to me." You are reading this book because deep inside, you want to achieve more. You know there is a better life waiting for you and you know that without change, commitment and action, nothing will happen. Tap into what motivates you and keep your eye on the prize! Be aware of the traps that will slow you or push you off course, or even make you want to abandon the cockpit and go back to being a Passenger. You'll be tempted — you're human. But you can resist and stay in the Pilot's seat. You have the power of choice.

Above all, remember that the desire to make big changes may be a radical, emotional "Aha!" moment, but change itself happens slowly and steadily. Give yourself a break, be patient, and keep fine-tuning your bearings and stay on track.

Everything starts with a thought, an idea ... a dream. Everything!

It took J.K. Rowling six years to write the first **Harry Potter** book. Olympic athletes work for years to become great, for them it starts with that dream of standing on the podium with a gold medal around their necks. Move backwards from there and you'll see years of repetitive, back-breaking training. Small measures and small changes, wrought consistently over time, can move mountains.

Plus, moving slowly gives you time to savour the journey, to stop and smell the roses. By celebrating the small wins and enjoying every step, you'll ensure that when you finally reach your goal, you'll be truly happy to be there.

Key Questions

- What end am I aiming for?
- In what timeframe?
- What factors related to my goals are in my control?
- Which ones are beyond my control and how can I work around them?
- How would I generally describe my self-talk? As positive and empowering or negative and helpless?
- What am I going to do to improve my self-talk?
- What's on my bucket list and when am I going to check them off?

The Million-Dollar Question

What is my "Why"? What is the underlying reason why I want to make changes in my life and career?

If the want is strong enough, the how will happen!

Your Brain Will Take You Where You Point It

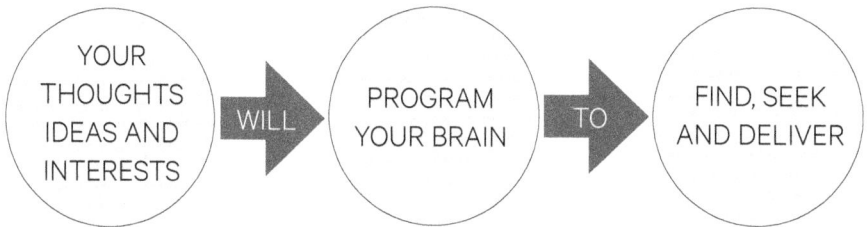

YOUR THOUGHTS IDEAS AND INTERESTS → WILL → PROGRAM YOUR BRAIN → TO → FIND, SEEK AND DELIVER

The subconscious mind is where all the real work happens — it never sleeps, processing your thoughts 24/7.

"The human brain had a vast memory storage. It made us curious and very creative. Those were the characteristics that gave us an advantage — curiosity, creativity and memory. And that brain did something very special. It invented an idea called 'the future.'"

—Dr. David Suzuki

I think it was Albert Einstein that once said, "The thoughts in your mind today are merely previews of the movies you'll star in tomorrow." How's that for a big idea to start a chapter? But it's true; everything starts with an idea, a "what if?" question. He also said, "We can't solve problems by using the same kind of thinking we used when we created them." So it follows that if you want your future to look differently from your life today — if you want the end to be what you only dream about now — you need to start by changing how you think.

So it follows that if you want your future to look differently from your life today — if you want the end to be what you only dream about now — you need to start by changing how you think.

Let's begin by taking a closer look at a common phrase: "pay attention". You've heard it a million times – or, if you were a distracted and curious child like I was, a billion times. But the phrase has a deeper meaning than a simple command to concentrate. When you want to make something happen, you must turn your attention to it. You can't write a report, make a sale or invent a microchip without focus. To get results, we literally have to *pay attention*. It keeps us alert and aware, and helps us play at the top of our game.

Attention is *currency* we use to buy the outcomes we desire.

But here's what's really interesting: we have a limited supply of attention. The fact is, you can only focus effectively on one thing at a time, although women are much better at multi-tasking than men. Try listening to two conversations at a party and hearing more than a few fragments of each. You can't do it. The brain simply isn't designed that way. We're only capable of focusing our attention on one subject at a time. Attention is precious, and so much hinges on how you spend your limited supply. What you pay attention to is what you will get.

Put it another way and you have Raw Fact #4:

Your brain will take you where you point it.

In other words, if you want to make happen the future you desire, you have to dedicate your attention to actions and outcomes that will make that future a reality. Whatever you choose to give your attention to will be what you get in the end. Do you spend hours watching television each day when you could be exercising and getting fit? That's why you have a potbelly instead of washboard abs! Do you waste your valuable attention complaining about your miserable job to your friends instead of carrying out your plans to start your own business? That's why you're still in that miserable job instead of working for yourself.

Where the brain goes, results follow. So, as we move beyond the gap between where you are and where you want to be, let's take a closer look at how you use your brain – and why.

Thoughts Are Habits

The brain is the most powerful tool in the world. Think of the space between your ears as the most valuable piece of real estate on the planet. You can develop it fully and beautifully, or you can allow people to dump their trash in it. If you had a block of land, how would you guard it against litter and squatters? Would you put a fence around it? Maybe, but you can't block out the entire world by building a

Think of the space between your ears as the most valuable piece of real estate on the planet. You can develop it fully and beautifully, or you can allow people to dump their trash in it.

fence around your consciousness. You can, however, develop better habits and more disciplined thinking.

The famous sixth-century Chinese philosopher Lao Tzu wrote: "Watch your thoughts. They become words. Watch your words. They become deeds. Watch your deeds. They become habits. Watch your habits. They become character. Character is everything." Truer words have rarely been spoken. Your thinking is a habit. What you dwell on, whether you find hope or hopelessness in situations, what you see in other people — it's all habitual behaviour, the stuff you choose to give your attention to. The good news is that habits can be broken and new habits can develop. The bad news? It's bloody hard work to break a lifelong habit.

Before the negative self-talk cuts in and you get disheartened and start to think this is all too difficult, I'd like to share with you three powerful points I picked up from an article written by a gentleman named James Clear on forming new habits. In it, he talks about studies that show it takes on average of 66 days to form a new habit, not two or three weeks as is often cited. He says:

Before you let this dishearten you, let's talk about three reasons why this research is actually inspiring.

First, there is no reason to get down on yourself if you try something for a few weeks and it doesn't become a habit. It's supposed to take longer than that! There is no need to judge yourself if you can't master a behaviour in 21 short days. Embrace the long, slow walk to greatness and focus on putting in your reps.

Second, you don't have to be perfect. Making a mistake once or twice has no measurable impact on your long-term habits. This is why you should treat failure like a scientist, give yourself permission to make mistakes, and develop strategies for getting back on track quickly.

And third, embracing longer timelines can help us realise that habits are a process and not an event. All of the "21 Days" hype can make it really easy to think, "Oh, I'll just do this and it'll be done." But habits never work that way. You have to embrace the process. You have to commit to the system.

Understanding this from the beginning makes it easier to manage your expectations and commit to making small, incremental improvements...

Firstly, you must acknowledge the power your habits have over you. The behaviours we engage in daily are what shape our lives. If you've been in the habit of going for a daily 10km run for the past 10 years, you're probably a very fit person. If you've been in the habit of eating junk food at every meal for the past decade, you're probably a fat slob. Habits shape everything about who we are and where we're going. You can gain power over them, but first you have to be aware of your own habitual patterns of thinking.

Metacognition = Conscious Awareness

The state of being consciously aware of one's own thinking is called *metacognition,* and it's one of the most valuable skills you can cultivate. Imagine part of your mind being able to stand back and watch the rest of your mind think. You could notice when you became angry over trifles or assess how you talk to your children about a discipline problem. You could catch yourself in anxious or negative thinking and change it. That's powerful stuff!

Metacognition guards your mind against negativity and defeating thoughts from the outside. You are more aware of unconscious modes of thought that hold you back: defeatism,

The state of being consciously aware of one's own thinking is called metacognition, and it's one of the most valuable skills you can cultivate.

pessimism, procrastination, excuses, blaming and so on. Think about it this way: you're trying to get your mind fit so you can create a champion future. Just as you train your body to be fit, you have to train your mind to be mentally fit. That means more exercise and less garbage. Metacognition helps you limit the amount of mental junk food you consume: negative individuals, trash media, idiotic books, films and video games, and the like. A bit of junk food is okay from time-to-time but you wouldn't want to live on it.

Just as you train your body to be fit, you have to train your mind to be mentally fit. That means more exercise and less garbage.

How can you develop this skill? Firstly, don't think you must become some sort of Zen master. I think one of the best ways to start being mindful of your own thoughts is to set an alarm on your smartphone. To start with, set it to go off every three hours. That alarm is your reminder to stop what you're doing and examine how you're thinking at that moment. What's going through your mind? Are your thoughts helpful to your development, harmful or neutral? The more you do this, the more you'll begin to see patterns in how you think and what those thoughts lead to. For example, if you regularly have bitterly self-critical thoughts followed by bouts of binge eating, that's something you need to address right away.

Once you've started to develop the habit of examining your thoughts, start asking why you engage in those thought patterns and **write your conclusions** in a journal. This is powerful. Why do you get angry at your mate or your spouse? Why do you have feelings of despair about your job? What's really going on? **Why** is the most important question we can ever ask, and when you start asking it consistently, you'll start seeing answers. They might not be comfortable answers, but they'll be real and they'll guide you to make important changes.

It sounds empowering, but let's be honest. You can't be mindful 100 per cent of the time. You're going to live by habit to some degree, no matter what you do. Make sure your habits serve your goals! Here are some ways to do that:

- **Visualisation.** What does your mind dwell on? Visualising what you want to achieve is like drawing a mind map on paper. You see what you want and synchronise your brain with that goal. This isn't mumbo jumbo; it's behavioural science. Elite athletes have engaged in this technique for many years with powerful results. If you can see a concrete goal in your mind, it becomes real to your brain. The brain cannot distinguish between purely mental phenomena and real things in physical space, so if you achieve your goal in your head, you're one step closer to achieving it in reality.

  You can't be mindful 100 per cent of the time. You're going to live by habit to some degree, no matter what you do. Make sure your habits serve your goals!

  To achieve the things you want in life, you have to be mindful of them. If you see yourself as being able to achieve success and being happy, you're more likely to go there. If the thought comes into your mind that you'll never have the job you want, your mind will lead you to that outcome. Your mind will sabotage you.

- **Affirmation.** Your daily word choices and thought patterns influence your self-image, how other people see you, and your unconscious behaviour. If you regularly denigrate yourself or say things such as, "I'm so stupid!" or "I don't have what takes to run a business", you know what? You're right. Changing your habitual self-talk is an effective way of changing your thoughts.

That's why I suggest that my audiences experiment with affirmations. I don't mean the airy-fairy kind, but specific affirmations about your future. Write several "power phrases" that apply to your goals, and at points throughout your day, repeat them quietly to yourself. For example:

- "I'm right where I need to be to start moving forward."
- "I own my space."
- "I have the brains and talent to create a better future."
- "My ideas are sound and worth developing."

Stay Out of the Matrix

The trouble is, as much as toxic people can fill our minds with negativity, we do as much damage to ourselves by embracing distracted, unconscious behaviour.

The trouble is, as much as toxic people can fill our minds with negativity, we do as much damage to ourselves by embracing distracted, unconscious behaviour. Modern culture is terribly afraid of mental silence; it's as though we fear what we'll hear inside our heads if we stop watching, listening and tweeting long enough to pay attention to our internal monologue. People say, "I have nothing to do." But we have been conditioned to believe that it's bad to sit quietly and reflect. Why? Is it too painful?

Welcome to the Matrix: a consequence of the media age that wants distracted, thoughtless consumers, not thoughtful actors. There's immense profit in keeping us distracted, docile and spending money. Hence the constant bombardment of information, misinformation, games, entertainment and scandal. No wonder it's so easy to click into "always on" mode. Those people you know who can't seem to stop checking Facebook, Twitter or text messages on their smartphones, who panic at the thought of being unplugged even for a few minutes – they're plugged into the Matrix.

The Matrix is the enemy of mindfulness, that metacognitive state I talked about earlier. It encourages us to not question our thoughts, to act reflexively instead of *reflectively*. For example, studies found that when Tiger Woods won a golf tournament, the US stock market went up the following day. Why? What does a pro golfer have to do with the market capitalisation of corporations? Nothing, but that's not the point. Generally speaking, stockbrokers and the like enjoy and follow golf. A US win lifted mood and spirit resulting in a positive market increase. So much of what happens is a reflection of what we unconsciously let in.

If you're going to point your brain towards your goal, unplug from the Matrix and stay unplugged. Teach yourself to be mindful of what's coming at you and what you let in. Guard your mind against gossip, small-mindedness and fear. Be mindful of what you want to achieve and your goals. Don't let just anything into your subconscious. Learn to develop a healthy and respectful scepticism.

Teach yourself to be mindful of what's coming at you and what you let in. Guard your mind against gossip, small-mindedness and fear.

I've found that one of the best ways to do this is to question your assumptions. Why do you do accept certain things as inevitable or as the only way to achieve a goal? The answers can be amazing. Personal example: years ago, I bought a house in a new estate with a lovely, large front lawn, just like all the other homes in the estate. And just like my neighbours, I became a slave to this lawn. I would fertilise it, weed it and water it like a loving parent. I spent a small fortune installing a state-of-the-art sprinkler system.

My lawn consumed a large part of my spare time, and a stack of money. Then we experienced a longterm drought and it became increasingly hard to maintain the lush lawn I loved. I decided it would make more sense for me to get rid of my lawn and re-landscape with a native garden. I would tear out the lawn, put in low water usage plants and create something that wouldn't require a lot of maintenance. I made a plan ... and did nothing. I was afraid to kill off such a beautiful lawn; afraid of what the neighbours might think, afraid that my grand plan might look like crap. Nine months passed, and still every week I would cut and trim and nurture my lawn. Finally, one Sunday afternoon after I had slavishly finished mowing the lawn, I was spraying weed killer on the paths, and I heard a little voice say to me: "Kill the lawn Alex If you don't, you are never going to change it." I assure you, I have never heard voices encouraging me to kill anyone or anything else. Honestly!

The little voice repeated the message: "Kill the lawn." In that moment, I pumped up my sprayer, had one last good look at the lawn and started walking back and forth, spraying weed killer from one corner to the other. I poisoned the daylights out of that lawn and, strangely, I was smiling. My neighbour Gary came over a week later to ask what was happening to my lawn. "It's going yellowish," he said with a hint of alarm. When I told him I'd poisoned it, he looked at me as though I was crazy.

A few weeks later, in came the soil, plants and chip bark for my lovely native garden. I planted it exactly as I had planned and imagined, and I've enjoyed it for the past 10 years. I trim it twice a year and rake the path once every few weeks. I've bought back about 120 hours a year of leisure time, all because I questioned my long-standing assumption that a green lawn was the only way to go and forced myself to act.

Think outside the square and question the norm. That's how you stay out of the Matrix. Use the "what if?" question as a constant source of inspiration and creativity.

I'll Stop Procrastinating Tomorrow

Apart from unconscious behaviour and unquestioning acceptance of assumptions, the other great enemy of mindfulness and attention is *procrastination.* Our culture of distraction isn't only about the avoidance of inner silence and contemplation; it's about wasting time and delaying action.

Our culture of distraction isn't only about the avoidance of inner silence and contemplation; it's about wasting time and delaying action.

Our world is filled to bursting with time black holes that rob us of the precious and finite resource called time: social networks, the media, the internet in general, television, sports, politics, advertising and more. Distractions are everywhere, every minute. It seems that everyone and everything is competing for our time. We complain about not having enough time, but that's not true. We all have 24 hours every day. We have enough time; we just don't *use* the time we have wisely. Instead of focusing our attention on a single goal and a tight group of actions designed to get us to that goal, we dabble and fool around with everything that allows us to do *nothing.* We promise we'll get to the important activities tomorrow ... only tomorrow never comes. Eventually, we run out of tomorrows. Sound familiar?

Why are we so good at procrastination? Because our brains evolved to protect us from foolish risks that might get us killed before we could bear children. That also means we gravitate towards the familiar, because our brains assume the known is safe. As a result, our brains look for every possible reason to procrastinate with familiar activities so we can avoid scary new activities. We also procrastinate because of laziness. We're comfortable with the status quo. We fear choice, because by picking one path or one item we automatically miss out on the ones we didn't pick. To make matters worse, in today's world of abundant information at the click of a mouse, we over-analyse. Too much information leads to "paralysis by analysis".

Successful people are the opposite of procrastinators. They are "initiators", people who take action quickly once the desire strikes. Often, it's because they've discovered the ultimate brain hack:

Successful people are the opposite of procrastinators. They are "initiators", people who take action quickly once the desire strikes.

If you act on an idea or desire now, before your brain can compel you to procrastinate, you're much more likely to follow through and use your time wisely.

In other words, when you take the initiative and act quickly, you don't give the "delay and wait" part of your mind a chance to drag you into your favourite chair to binge-watch your favourite TV series. When you have a strong desire for what you want, taking fast action feels great. It feels better than being a sloth lying around the house in your sweatpants, eating pizza. Knowing precisely what you desire most —and what activities will bring you closer to it — is one powerful brain hack!

Here's another: remove opportunities to procrastinate ahead of time. You'll make it easier to get into new habits! Track how much time you waste on distractions and put them out of reach. It's like losing weight. Would you rather pack your kitchen full of fattening food and rely on your willpower to not eat it, or make it as hard as possible to cheat? There are no points for form; results are what matter. Do whatever you must to force yourself into new habits.

The Opportunities Were Always There

One of the questions I'm often asked when I give this part of my talk is: "Alex, how do we know what we're supposed to focus our attention on?" People get confused. When they shed distraction and become mindful of their thoughts, they're unsure where to go next. Where do you point your brain when you're unsure where you want to go?

Here's a reasonably stunning piece of information I discovered a few years ago on my own journey:

> *The opportunities you've been waiting for*
> *have always been waiting for YOU.*

There's an extraordinary part of the brain called the *reticular activating system,* or RAS. Its basic, boring purpose is to regulate your sleep-wake cycle, but it also has an off-label function that's key to what we're talking about. The RAS serves as a relevance filter, like a radar that only picks up what's important to you. Think of the last time you got a new car. While driving your sleek new object of desire home, you probably suddenly noticed dozens of the exact same car. Did you spark some sort of run on that particular model?

No, of course not. Your RAS is on full alert, filtering unimportant input to draw your attention only to things that matter to you — in this case, cars such as the shiny new baby you just bought. Before you bought your MG convertible, those other MGs were always on the road. You just didn't notice them. The same effect is in play when you're in an airport. Despite the cacophony, you'll hear sounds that concern you, such as your name being called over the public address system. Why? Because your name or flight number is important to you. All the other announcements are just background clutter.

The same principle applies to opportunities in life. Positive people look for ways of changing for the better, new jobs or business ideas — they have always been all around you; you just didn't perceive them. There's no need to go to the ends of the Earth on some heroic quest for your life's purpose or future plans. They're around you, and if they're not in your hometown, they're probably nearby. All you have to do is open yourself up to them.

The sheer act of telling your brain what you're looking for and making those things important will change how you perceive the world. For example, if you decide that the thing you want most — the future that lies on the other side of your gap — is owning your own chain of restaurants, your attention and focus will be transformed instantly. You'll start to notice articles in the paper on topics relevant to your goal, such as culinary and restaurant management classes and trends in dining. You'll hear people talking about things you care about, from small business loans to restaurant marketing.

There's an old saying: "Luck favours the prepared." When you're prepared to notice and capitalise on opportunities, you'll be shocked at how lucky you become.

It will seem like the most incredible coincidence, but don't be fooled. The reality is more marvellous: these things were always there! By re-orienting your mind on what you want, you unlock this previously hidden resource: a gold mine of financing, expertise, information and allies. It's not luck, either. There's an old saying: "Luck favours the prepared." When you're prepared to notice and capitalise on opportunities, you'll be shocked at how lucky you become.

Pointing Your Brain in the Right Direction

Take what's fascinating and irresistible to you today and point your attention towards it. Let the car roll downhill and pick up speed. As you do, you'll start to get information and learn more about the topic. If it's something you should pursue for the long term, one day you'll have an *activating event*, a moment that changes everything, where thoughts and attention become decisions and action. You'll know that's where you want your brain to take you.

There's no predicting an activating event, but you can put yourself in proximity to one, such as standing next to the tracks if you want to catch a train. You might not catch one right away, but you've got a much better chance than if you stand in an open field!

Your brain has extraordinary power. Clear away the clutter, let it see clearly, and it will lead you where you want to go. Remember:

If the want is strong enough, the how will happen.

The Million-Dollar Question

*What's most important to me? What are the details
— how I'll get there, what it will look and feel like
when I do, and how the journey will change me?*

107

Think Like a Child and Open Your Mind

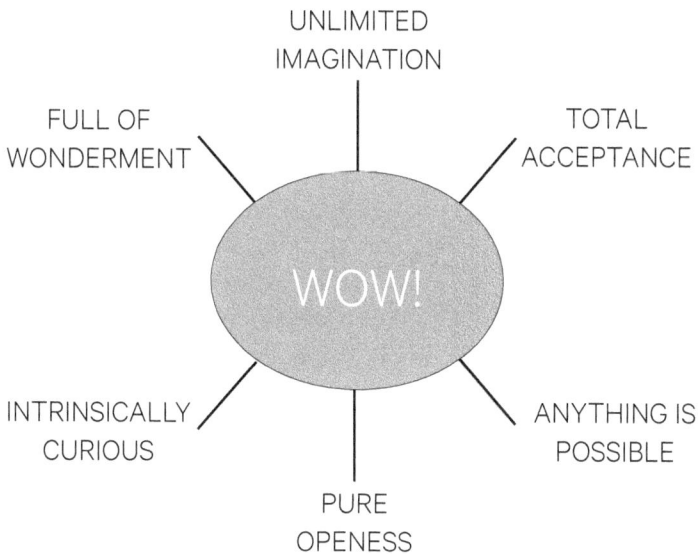

UNLIMITED
IMAGINATION

FULL OF
WONDERMENT

TOTAL
ACCEPTANCE

WOW!

INTRINSICALLY
CURIOUS

ANYTHING IS
POSSIBLE

PURE
OPENESS

Life through the eyes of a five-year-old
is AWESOME!

*"Children are smarter than any of us. Know how I
know that? I don't know one child with a full-time
job and children."*

—Bill Hicks, comedian

When I was 29 years old, we sold off the fresh-food chain we had created over the past five years and I joined Ampol Road Pantry as a Franchise Business Advisor. I'd had a successful career in the grocery industry and I'd learnt a huge lesson from my disastrous first sojourn into small business. After that, I regrouped and helped create the SFM chain, the second-largest fresh-food chain in Australia, and I was feeling pretty good about myself. Once again, I thought I knew it all ... and then I met Bob Bailey. Bob was my general manager, and little did I know how much of an influence this man would have on my life.

Bob was based in Albury, about a three-hour drive from Melbourne. During the first few months on the job, I only spent a small amount of time with Bob. Our career backgrounds had several similarities. Bob grew up working in his father's "butchercatessen": a term he coined for a combined butcher shop and delicatessen. He finished school and became a butcher, working in the family business before moving into the supermarket industry. Finally, after some ups and downs — and with the support of his amazing wife, Jill — he acquired and ran a chain of independent supermarkets, sold all but two of them and joined Ampol Road Pantry as their National Marketing Manager and later took over the role of General Manager. He was truly a self-made man.

Bob is an amazing character; likeable, full of energy, astute, and with the ability to connect well with people. He is very successful yet deeply grounded. About three months after I started with the company, Bob called me to let me know that he was coming to Melbourne. He said, "AB, I'm flying into Melbourne tonight. How about we catch up for a chop?" Trying hard not to sound stupid, I tried to work out what he was talking about. A chop? What the hell was that? Luckily, then he said he knew a nice restaurant close to his hotel, and the penny dropped. "Catching up for a chop" was Bob's way of inviting me to dinner.

"That would be great," I replied, and we planned to meet at 7pm. I got off the phone feeling like an excited and confused school kid. Dinner with the GM — just Bob and me! This would be my opportunity to strut my stuff and impress him with my vast knowledge of retail.

We met at a nice restaurant and had a terrific meal. We talked about all sorts of things, shared supermarket tales, butcher's jokes and even business stories. I thought we were getting on very well: Bob felt like a father figure, it was great talking him, and I was on fire. Then as we were having a "cleansing ale" (Bob's term for the last beer of the night), he leaned back, looked at me and slowly said, "AB, I think I can make something out of you as long as you can accept these two things: you know nothing, and the little bit you think you know is wrong! Reckon you can handle that?"

I was gobsmacked! I'm sure the look on my face was priceless. It was like he was asking me to swallow a baseball. He looked me in the eye and repeated it again, word for word. I stammered and "ummed", and when I finally got my head and mouth synchronised, I asked: "What do you mean?" And then came the single most important lesson I have ever been given.

Bob said to me, "If you think you know it all, you'll miss it all. You see, when you think you know everything, you'll never learn anything. All night you have been telling me what you've achieved, how you know this and you know that. When I started talking about something, you hijacked the conversation to show me how much you know. You're too busy talking to listen and you're too afraid to admit when you don't know something."

"You see, when you think you know everything, you'll never learn anything ..."

Boy, I was listening now! I knew that Bob was telling me this from a good space. He wasn't tearing me down or berating me. His tonality was a cross between a school principal and a caring farther. And the reality was I knew he was absolutely right. It struck me that during our dinner, when Bob asked about a subject, I leapt at the chance to show him how much I knew about it and how brilliant I was. But what I was really showing him was how little I listened or paid attention. The message was pretty simple:

If you think you know it all, you miss it all.

And, if you really want to start learning,
start thinking like a child again.

You see, five year olds have no ego. Everything is possible, everything's exciting. A five year old is constantly curious: "Why? Why not? What's this?" Five year olds are sponges taking in information and experiences through all their senses – sight, sound, touch, taste and smell — absorbing and learning at an incredible rate. A five year old might not know the mechanics behind what they're seeing, but they know it's amazing and worth investigating. There's a reason why children love pretending to be detectives and explorers: they're naturals at asking questions and discovering answers.

That's what Bob was asking me if I could do. Could I set aside my ego — a tough thing for any 29 year old to do — and see everything as though it was new, without any preconceptions? Could I accept my ignorance and open myself to total learning? For a moment, I wasn't sure. Then I looked at Bob and said with a confidence I did not feel, "Bob, I can." That would be the beginning of one of the most challenging, most rewarding periods in my life.

Everything's a Wonderment

If you've gotten this far in this book, odds are you've at least begun to look at your gap, figure out what's important to you and point your attention towards what you want to achieve. Now the obvious question is: "How do I sustain the new type of thinking I'll need in order to get somewhere I've never been before?"

My answer is to think like a child. Re-awaken your curiosity and discard everything you think you know. Let go of "seen it all" cynicism and the need to be the smartest person in the room. I did that and it changed everything about how I think and how I look at learning.

My answer is to think like a child. Re-awaken your curiosity and discard everything you think you know.

Unfortunately, by the time we become adults, family, friends, teachers and the media have often conditioned us to stop asking and learning – as mentioned earlier in the book. The first five years of life are pure intake. Being a five year old is awesome! But then we start school and the real conditioning starts. We're told what to read, how to sit, what to do and what not to do. There's nothing wrong with those things; everyone needs to learn basic skills and how to fit into society. But we also learn what it means to be embarrassed. We learn not to think outside the box because we'll be laughed at, and our parents will be told that we're "different". Slowly, starting in primary school and continuing through university, we're funneled through a system that's designed to qualify us for a job — not to learn how to think. Even university, which is supposed to be a laboratory of challenge and questioning, is awash with conformity.

Friends, relatives, family and teachers—they all do it because they love us and don't want to see us get hurt. They know that in a conformist world, people who ask awkward questions and challenge conventional wisdom are often scorned and mocked.

Modern culture encourages us to accept certain things as gospel. That's what makes a good consumer and a compliant citizen. Instead of questioning and asking, we pretend we know what we're doing. If we do ask about something that shouldn't be asked about, others say: "That's a silly question." We become jaded. Even if our income grows, our spirit shrinks. We're lost in the Matrix, just another unquestioning drone following the program.

*Assume you don't know **anything** so that you can be open to **everything**. As you move into an unknown future towards your end goals, you'll have to venture into unknown areas of knowledge.*

Scientists, however, think like children. They don't accept that the sky is blue; they ask why it is blue and figure out the optical principles that make it appear blue to our eyes. That's what I mean by thinking like a child. Assume you don't know *anything* so that you can be open to *everything*. As you move into an unknown future towards your end goals, you'll have to venture into unknown areas of knowledge. To do that, you need total, childlike curiosity.

If you want to change how you think, start by making "why", "how" and "what if" questions a natural part of your daily life. Because:

If you're not learning, you're not growing.
If you're not growing, you're dying!

Start With "I Don't Know"

You know what personal growth's public enemy number one is? *Misplaced certainty*. There's nothing more corrosive. If we think we know everything already, we make ourselves dumber. We become dogmatic, even evangelical, in our ignorance. It becomes more important to be right than to be enlightened.

Explorers are willing to say, "I don't know." So are confident, successful people. It's only the insecure ones who have to impress everyone in the room with how much they know, what they've done and where they've been. Those kinds of people are hard to work with, and not just because they're insufferable know-it-alls, but because their insistence on pretending to know everything makes them the most likely ones to drop the ball on a big project or make a mistake that drives away a potential customer or client. They are so hell-bent on appearing smart that they don't listen, and it makes them seem arrogant, disinterested and stupid. I call them "dinosaurs" because they're destined for extinction!

I've sat through (read: suffered through) my share of high-level corporate meetings, and it's astonishing how invested everyone is in pretending to have all the answers – that is, until someone confesses that they don't. I recall one particular management meeting where the chief financial officer presented a series of complex financial scenarios to the senior management team. And, I just wasn't getting it. What was projected on the slides may as well have been nuclear physics equations. I was the youngest executive, and looking around the room all I could see were very serious-looking, silver-haired gentlemen in suits, nodding and pretending everything was crystal clear. However, their eyes said it all: they weren't getting it either.

I've sat through my share of high-level corporate meetings, and it's astonishing how invested everyone is in pretending to have all the answers – that is, until someone confesses that they don't.

So I used my favourite line. I piped up and said, "Excuse me, Stephen. I'm a bit thick today, and I'm just not getting it. Could you run through it again from the top in layman's terms?"

The moment I did that, every other head in that room started nodding! *Every one.* Everyone else was having as hard a time following the presentation as I was, but they were too invested in the need to seem brilliant to ask a simple question. No one wants to say, "I don't know," but the moment one does, it frees everybody else to confess his own ignorance. Beware of "groupthink".

The other example that comes to mind: I was at a private, 16-guest dinner at one of Melbourne's finest hotels, celebrating the inaugural grand prix in Melbourne. We were the guests of a tobacco company, so as you can imagine, money was not a barrier. We had a private room and were seated at a large boardroom-style table with all the finery and crystal you could imagine. The maître'd presented us with a leather-bound, handwritten menu, while four waiters moved from their respective corners and poured vintage wine. This was all very impressive — however, the beautifully bound parchment menus were written in French! The other guests were looking at their menus and made the right noises: "Hmm" and "Oh yes." I thought I was the only one at the table who couldn't read or understand French!

Finally, concerned that I would order a main serving of mustard, I asked one of the waiters to walk me through the menu. Instantly, there was an audible, collective sigh of relief from around the table. Comments such as, "Yes, that would be great," and, "I thought I was the only one," broke the group into embarrassed laughter as the wait staff kindly walked us through the menu. It was as though one person admitting he didn't read French gave the entire group permission to do the same.

Everyone was in the same boat but no one was prepared to admit it for fear of looking stupid. We fear being ridiculed, and we hate being embarrassed or made to look stupid. Humans have a herd mentality; when someone strays from the herd, they are vulnerable to predators. But this mindset severely limits not only what we can learn, but how much we can enjoy things, such as a sumptuous meal.

Challenge your own herd mentality. Don't be afraid to admit you don't understand something. It's the only way you'll learn. It can also be enlightening to ask someone to explain something and discover that they don't know, either! Great success stories come from people willing to be mocked or ridiculed. Einstein was ridiculed. Gandhi was ridiculed. Mandela was ridiculed, thrown in prison and then ridiculed some more. It's practically a law of nature that if you're trying to bring about radical change or develop a wildly new idea, you're going to be laughed at, ridiculed or met with scorn. We're conditioned to conform.

If you want to strike out on your path and take the controls in the pilot's seat, you've got to make the saying "I don't know, but I'm going to find out" a habit. You've got to be as open and questioning as a child — drop your ego and break that lifetime of conditioning and be willing to look thick. Don't get me wrong; this is not easy. As you grow, people will resist you leaving the herd. They might be protecting you because they care about you and don't want you to be made a fool of, or because they don't want you leaving their comfortable circle.

Being mocked and being uncomfortable is a rite of passage. If you're not being made sport of for asking "silly" questions, you're playing it too safe and will never get where you want to be.

Being mocked and being uncomfortable is a rite of passage. If you're not being made sport of for asking "silly" questions, you're playing it too safe.

80-20 Rule

In fact, I would go so far as to say that the more people laughing at you, ridiculing your ideas or admonishing you for asking questions, the more you are on the road to success. You're thinking originally. This is where the "80-20 Rule" comes into play. If you're not familiar with it, the 80/20 Rule, known as the Pereto Principle, is also called the "Law of the Vital Few". According to this law, only 20 per cent of the population produces the innovations and daring ideas that determine how the other 80 per cent lives. The majority influences the minority, but the minority reshapes the world. Everything starts with a daring, original, disruptive thought, and only the 20 per cent that breaks from the herd is even *capable* of such thoughts.

By way of an example, a question: when you feed your dog, do you give it table scraps? Probably not. More than likely, you give your pooch dog food from a can. Well, it wasn't always that way. Before World War II, people fed their dogs scraps. A while back, I met a man whose father's best mate changed that. The man came up with an idea while living on cans of "bully beef" during World War II. He asked himself: "What if dog food could be sold in cans so it could be stored without spoiling?" People laughed and said the idea was ridiculous. "Who would pay for dog food in a can?" In 2013, global canned dog food sales exceeded $13 billion. That's just one "silly idea", amongst millions of others, that's done pretty well.

Children don't care if their ideas are seen as crazy, so they don't self-edit. If you want to achieve great things, cultivate that same mentality.

Children don't care if their ideas are seen as crazy, so they don't self-edit. If you want to achieve great things, cultivate that same mentality. That doesn't mean that any idea that's ridiculed is automatically guaranteed to make you a millionaire; some ideas are mocked or misunderstood because they're not good. The trick is to keep pushing the boundaries in the face of laughter as you **begin** to explore your ideas. It's possible that, after some development, an idea for a business or product might not work out. So what? You cast it aside or file it for later use and move to the next one.

Remember, nothing is a self-evident success immediately. If you're truly outside your comfort zone, you're going to fail as often as you succeed. And that's okay. Imagine what the world would look like if we all gave up trying to walk the first time we tried because we fell over and banged our heads!

The secret to making progress lies in how you frame your failures. Are they examples of your incompetence, or are they inevitable road kill on the highway of life? Are failures belly wounds or just the fallout from grand experiments where the beaker blew up in your hands? Is your response to an idea falling flat, "Damn, I don't know if I can do this again," or, "Okay, I took my best shot, what did I learn and what's next?" Remember an old saying:

The secret to making progress lies in how you frame your failures. Are they examples of your incompetence, or are they inevitable road kill on the highway of life?

> *The turtle only makes progress when it sticks its neck out.*

You get nowhere without sticking your toe in the water. The most successful, wealthy people I know have many toes in the water, testing multiple new ideas for companies, products, life directions or creative projects. Some work, others don't. But they have no fear about testing the waters. They are perpetual children, approaching every "what if?" with enthusiasm, wonder and a sense of possibility. That's true for entrepreneurs, artists and anyone in any field who wants to blaze a new trail through previously uncharted territory.

There's a simple but profound difference in the mentality of those who keep finding new wonders to chase and ideas to develop and those who give up after a few setbacks:

Those who stop are the ones who ask, "Why?"

Those who stop are the ones who ask, "Why?"

Those who persist are the ones who ask, "Why not?"

Those who persist are the ones who ask, "Why not?"

Which are you today? Which will you be tomorrow?

"No-Proofing" Yourself

Childlike thinkers avoid "can't" in their self-talk. They also develop a firm resistance to the word "no". They revel in hearing "you can't" from others because it makes them try even harder, but they are careful to avoid using the word themselves because it functions like a "delete" key in their subconscious mind. If you say, "I can't do that," your brain will say, "Okay, next!"

Don't shut down your possibilities. You will get enough of that from other people. They will attempt to shut down your most imaginative thinking because, again, they fear what's outside the norm. But it's more than that. If they're not creative or courageous themselves, your creative, investigative fire shines a light on their own failures. If someone tries to talk you out of your dream, you can bet it's because they cast an unflattering shadow in its glow.

"No-proofing" yourself is a key part of the Pilot or Passenger mindset. However, you need two kinds of mental armour:

1. Imperviousness to the outside world telling you what you can't do.

2. Deafness to that nagging voice in your head that says, "You're not good enough", or, "This is never going to work."

Listening to either one will shut you down in a heartbeat or wear you down over time. If you're not *really* convinced that you can come up with a new product, publish a fresh kind of fiction or plan and set off on your path to live the life you deserve, you may be subconsciously looking for the outside "no" as an excuse to say, "No, you're right, I can't do this."

It's important to be mindful of your internal self-talk, because your resistance to your own doubts determines your resistance to the doubts of others. How strong is your belief in your ability to break new ground? How strongly do you rely on others' approval to progress towards your goals?

How strong is your belief in your ability to break new ground? How strongly do you rely on others' approval to progress towards your goals?

Negative Capability

Your answers will determine not only what is possible for you, but also what is *probable*. Part of your journey's wisdom lies in learning the difference between the two. Success demands more than stubbornly trudging towards any outcome. Part of success also means knowing when an outcome is so unlikely that it will drain the resources you could be using to achieve other marvellous outcomes. The 80/20 Rule applies here, too: 20 per cent of your activities will account for 80 per cent of your happiness. Also, 20 per cent of your actions will produce 80 per cent of your outcomes.

However, "possible" will never become "probable" until you can master that childlike way of looking at the world. Children see what adults don't. They are pure input. They're not judgemental.

They are completely present in the moment. There are no rules, no established mandates. There are no secret meanings behind accomplishments or failures.

Poet John Keats had a term for this: **negative capability**. He used it to explain why William Shakespeare was the greatest writer of all time. Negative capability is the ability to take in all sides of a situation or argument without coming to judgment — "hovering", as it were, between opposing poles without imposing your own biases or preconceptions on the situation. Shakespeare was a master at this, rarely tipping his hand about a character's motivations or actions and letting things resolve in real time.

Think like a juror in a courtroom, taking in information but not drawing premature conclusions. You'll be amazed at what you see.

If you want to look at the world as a child does, develop your own negative capability. It's natural to come into a situation and quickly pass judgment. Resist that temptation. Start training your mind to come to no preconceived judgements. Think like a juror in a courtroom, taking in information but not drawing premature conclusions. You'll be amazed at what you see.

Think Around Corners

Bicycling through the Tuscan countryside in 1895, Albert Einstein looked at the dappled light filtering through the trees and had a titanic thought: **What would the world look like if you could travel on a wave of light?** Many of us mere mortals would have dismissed such a thought with a shrug and gone on to more prosaic pursuits, such as food and fine wines. But Einstein possessed that rare combination of a dreamer's vision and insatiable curiosity. He took the question further: **Why is the speed of light so strange?**

He thought about an odd conundrum: if a cyclist pedalled directly towards you at 20 kilometres an hour, why wouldn't his image — the light reflected off his body and bicycle — reach you before he and his bike did? In other words, why couldn't you add the speed of a moving object to the speed of its light? Again, you or I might answer, "Well, it just is." But that wasn't enough for Albert. He delved deeper, and his answer changed the world. Very simply put, the speed of light is an absolute. It always travels at the same speed, no matter how fast the object the light comes from is moving.

Einstein did what I call "thinking around corners". It means asking questions, taking nothing for granted and looking beyond the obvious. It means willing to sound foolish by asking "why" about something that everyone else accepts without question. It's an essential skill: some of the best business ideas I've ever heard have come from some of my 15- and 16-year-old employees, who haven't been exposed to the conformist pressure of an organisation. They will look at something that's been done one way for years and ask: "Why do we do it that way?" Looking at it through new and innocent eyes, they'll suggest a new way of making widgets or communicating with customers that stops even the most senior people in their tracks.

Einstein did what I call "thinking around corners". It means asking questions, taking nothing for granted and looking beyond the obvious.

You can see the thoughts swirling in the heads of embarrassed senior managers, something to the effect of, "Why didn't I think of that?" Because you couldn't! If you rush to judgement or don't ask why, you're incapable of thinking around corners, of seeing things with fresh eyes. If you want to avoid that fate, consider taking definitive action.

Your values and beliefs about yourself are products of your environment. They determine your thoughts, and your thoughts manifest in your behaviour. If you want to change your behaviour, first rebuild your beliefs about what you're capable of.

Firstly, ask yourself how you've been conditioned and how that conditioning manifests in what you say, think and do. Conditioning is a product of your cumulative experiences. Think about the negative or limiting beliefs you have about yourself; list them on paper. Now put on your barrister's wig and dismantle the legs that support those beliefs. Where's your evidence? Once you've torn those beliefs apart, use positive points of reference to build a new set of positive "can-do" beliefs about yourself.

Start by asking important questions:

- What has influenced me to think and behave as I do?
- Are my responses to new ideas my own or have they been conditioned into me by parents, teachers and colleagues?
- Do I "respond" or "react" to situations?
- Are my responses likely to lead to the life and career I want?
- If not, then how do my responses need to change and what influences do I need to eliminate?

We've discussed getting negative people and mental junk food out of your life, and this is the same thing. If there are radio programs, periodicals, television shows, blogs or individuals who foster your unquestioning or conformist mindset, it's time to wave farewell to them forever.

Secondly, set out to change your thoughts and beliefs. Your actions stem from thoughts, and thoughts rise from your beliefs and conditioning. Everyone has an "inner child"; a blank-slate self, innocent, always looking for patterns, questioning everything and taking nothing for granted. But as we get older, some of us adopt the belief that we have to **know** things. Being right becomes the linchpin of our self-esteem. That's why so many people are willing to believe in extremist political and religious ideologies: doing so gives them the pleasure of being "right". It's also why contradicting such closely held beliefs often results in cognitive dissonance and anger: many of us link our self-worth to being right.

If you're going to make the leap to think around corners and see problems with fresh eyes, you must challenge your beliefs about why it's so important to be right. Can you train your belief system to take pleasure in asking questions and challenging the status quo? Can you find pride and self-esteem in becoming an explorer, someone who sends up trial balloons of new ideas and doesn't worry if some of them come crashing back to earth?

I believe you can. If you couldn't, you wouldn't have read this far.

Being right becomes the linchpin of our self-esteem. That's why so many people are willing to believe in extremist political and religious ideologies: doing so gives them the pleasure of being "right".

Key Questions

- How am I conditioned to view the new and unusual?
- How am I conditioned to respond to things that confirm my current beliefs?
- How did I become conditioned?
- Does my conditioning contradict my values or goals?
- Am I more likely to ask why or why not?
- What factors in my life influence me to conform?
- What new influences should I look for?
- What are the new questions I should be asking?

The Million-Dollar Question

Am I conditioned to believe that my self-worth comes from being right or from being daring and trying new things? If my belief doesn't serve my long-term goal, how can I challenge and change it?

You Can Lie to Others, But Don't Lie to Yourself

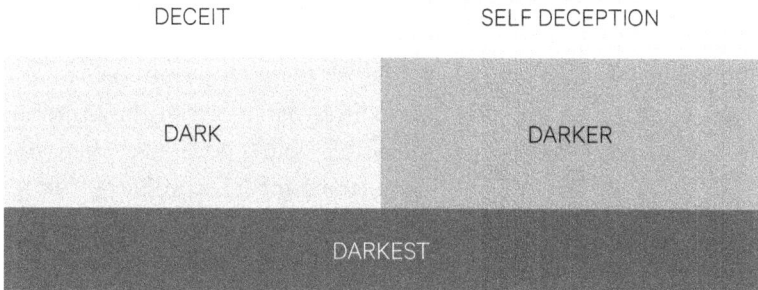

DECEIT	SELF DECEPTION
DARK	DARKER
DARKEST	

"Stop lying to yourself. When we deny our own truth, we deny our own potential."

— Steve Maraboli

"Most of our platitudes notwithstanding, self-deception remains the most difficult deception. The tricks that work on others count for nothing in that very well-lit back alley where one keeps assignations with oneself: no winning smiles will do here, no prettily drawn lists of good intentions."

—Joan Didion, Slouching Towards Bethlehem

In *Hamlet*, the character Polonius tells his son memorably, "This above all, to thine own self be true." That doesn't simply mean to stand by your values and act according to your own moral code, although that is extremely important. It also means that if you are going to be your best, you can't believe things about yourself that simply are not true. I'll go so far as to say this:

Self-deception, not gold, is the root of all evil.

There are people who will insist that people who pump themselves up with "I'm the one" talk and who "fake it till they make it" are happier and more successful than those who accept life at face value. That may be true, but that's not the kind of self-deception I'm talking about. I'm talking about the dangerous rationalisations, excuses and blaming we concoct in order to avoid the crippling guilt that can come with knowing we've gone off track in life – *and it's our fault*.

Human beings are so good at dodging responsibility that when we encounter someone who's honest about their terrible choices, we're taken aback. This is demonstrated in this wonderful story from an article written by American university professor Lloyd H. Steffen:

Once when Frederick II, an 18th-century king of Prussia, went on an inspection tour of a Berlin prison, he was greeted with the cries of prisoners, who fell on their knees and protested their unjust imprisonment. While listening to these pleas of innocence, Frederick's eye was caught by a solitary figure in the corner, a prisoner seemingly unconcerned with all the commotion.

"Why are you here?" Frederick asked him.

"Armed robbery, Your Majesty."

"Were you guilty?" the king asked.

"Oh yes, indeed, Your Majesty. I entirely deserve my punishment."

At that Frederick summoned the jailer. "Release this guilty man at once," he said. "I will not have him kept in this prison where he will corrupt all the fine innocent people who occupy it."

Amusing, but instructive, too. You have to wonder how many of those men shouting about their innocence had done nothing wrong. Few, I'll bet. But what's really interesting is that the king recognised that the ability to see and admit to one's shortcomings is a greater virtue than being oblivious to them. We're all flawed. We're all lazy, cruel, foolish or malicious from time to time. As an old saying goes, "The man who has no regrets for making a terrible mistake simply hasn't gotten around to making it yet."

That brings me to Raw Fact #6:

You can lie to others, but not to yourself.

We all have stories we tell ourselves about ourselves. They're stories in which we explain why our lives are like they are — what happened, why and who's responsible. That's normal and healthy; we all need a narrative to give us a frame through which we can see ourselves, and everyone embellishes the truth from time to time. The problem comes when the story, to speak plainly, is a lie. When we concoct a story without trying to understand our mistakes and learn from them, instead ducking responsibility or pretending they didn't happen, we don't grow. Worse yet, we set ourselves up to make the same mistakes all over again.

Everybody Has a Story

A friend once told me that people are like peaches: beautiful on the outside, with a rough, knurly nut in the middle. The flesh is a layer of stories – the ego – designed to protect that crazy, warty, ugly nut. The nut is the real us; the truth about who we are, what we fear, what we crave and what we obsess over. With this analogy, what's really important to remember is that peaches bruise easily. That's why so many people hate others questioning their story. When challenged, the peach (ego) is likely to get bruised.

A friend once told me that people are like peaches: beautiful on the outside, with a rough, knurly nut in the middle.

We're all fragile and we all want to be loved and respected. But some of us don't love and respect ourselves. When your self-esteem is bruised, you can't admit to your mistakes, bad choices and betrayals. *If I'm not perfect*, says the unhealthy thought process, *I'm not worth anything*. Unable to face our blunders and the regrets that come with them, we put cloths over the mirrors in our homes, make up a story and blame the world for our plight:

- It was somebody else's fault.
- It was bad luck.
- It was my idea and they stole it.
- If I had another chance, I would do things differently.
- The problem is with them, not with me.

The thing is, we all have a "nut" inside us. It's the real us, the culmination of all our experiences, lessons, trials and tribulations, successes and failures, laughter and joy, pleasure and pain. These shape our beliefs about ourselves, which in turn shape our attitudes and patterns of thinking, which ultimately drive our choices and behaviour.

Your story is what you use to explain how your "nut" got that way. If the story is true, you're probably taking responsibility for your errors and for actions that had negative consequences. You don't shy away from what happened or your role in it. As a result, you learn and grow. You get wiser through experience. You discover that failure isn't the end of the world and you have the strength to bounce. Your self-esteem is healthy. You're in the Pilot's seat.

On the other hand, if you use your story to rationalise what you have or haven't done in your life, you're probably avoiding facing up to your mistakes. You won't accept that you're the reason why you dropped your goals or allowed another year to pass by without any positive change in your world. The failure of your company or marriage? Gaining 25kg and developing high blood pressure? All someone else's fault.

Investing in a story that's a lie has many problems. First of all, you stop learning and growing. You stop dead in your tracks. Unexamined mistakes are repeated mistakes. You won't face your culpability in the wreckage of your dreams, so you're powerless to repair it. You have weak self-esteem and almost no power to recover when life knocks you down. What's worse, everybody knows your story is a false rationalisation except you. It's probably cost you jobs and relationships – and you don't even know it because you were blaming others!

If self-deception is so obvious and detrimental, why do we do it? As with many things, it becomes a habitual way to impress others and ease our pain. When two people meet, they present their peaches and exchange "ego stories". Over time, if a friendship develops, they start dropping their egos and begin to share more and more of the truth. However, we only ever really drop our egos and share the real us — the real story hidden in the "nut" — with a handful of people. Everyone else gets the exaggerated, rationalised or selective ego stories. After a while, we start to believe it ourselves.

The majority of people are dissatisfied with their lives, but not unhappy enough to do something positive to change them. It's much easier to sit in the back of the plane and swap stories with other Passengers than it is to become the Pilot.

The majority of people are dissatisfied with their lives, but not unhappy enough to do something positive to change them. It's much easier to sit in the back of the plane and swap stories with other Passengers than it is to become the Pilot.

The majority of people live in a world of resigned acceptance. To make their position more palatable, they use their story to deflect responsibility, deaden the pain of the truth, conceal their shortcomings or make themselves look good by creating a fantasy world of achievement.

We have a society of men and women who, in their own minds, have no need to change anything about who they are or how they behave. Why should they? According to their stories, they were on the verge of huge success when fate robbed them of it. Behind the scenes, their finances may be a disaster, but in public they drive a Ferrari and wear a Rolex watch. They are always "this close" to finishing that bestselling novel or starting their technology company — and when nothing happens, they have loads of reasons to explain why.

There's no need to learn, change or evolve, because they've deluded themselves into believing they're not responsible for their problems or that the problems don't exist. They choose to be blind, deaf and dumb to reality.

Perpetual Victims

You have probably met or heard of people like this. They repeat their story so many times, their fantasy becomes their reality. The ego protects us from pain, so it creates elaborate excuses for the things in our lives that aren't quite right: "Yeah, I don't care that I got the sack, I was going to leave anyway and the boss was a real goose!" "It wasn't my fault! I was texting on my mobile phone, but that stupid pedestrian should have seen me coming. Now I have to get the car fixed and get a new windscreen!"

> *The ego protects us from pain, so it creates elaborate excuses for the things in our lives that aren't quite right...*

Sometimes we tell ourselves some *amazing* lies in order to hide from ourselves. One of my favourites is: "I've been doing this stupid job for five years. If I had a better job, I could afford to go on a real holiday, but there's none out there!" Then there's: "No point saving. It doesn't matter how much I save, house prices just keep going up and I'll never be able to buy one!"

Most people who are tippy-toeing through life safely to death take on a victim mentality to cover their refusal to take ownership of their choices. When I hear people saying such things, I feel like giving them a sharp slap to the back of the head as a wake-up call. Remember: *we have choice.* You can choose to take stock, take ownership and take the controls.

Remember this mantra: "I don't know how I'm going to _____ but I'm going to find a way!" You fill in the blank. Repeat this over and over and you will soon find options and opportunities

If It's to Be, It's up to Me!

Back in 1978, when I was just 18 years old, a store manager named Stan Dakowie handed me a sheet of paper. He said to me, "Young Alex, here are a few golden tips if you really want to be a star." I still reflect on the contents of that paper and have shared them with thousands of people. What Stan handed to me were simple yet empowering statements, and you could do a lot worse than to make a copy of them and put it on your wall as a constant reminder.

This is what Stan gave me. Thanks, Stan, wherever you are.

Here's a tip...

If you want to be considered a star,

NEVER SAY THESE THINGS:

- *"They didn't get back to me" or "They're getting back to me." Both are equally disastrous. Expecting someone to get back to you stops the action. Take the initiative and keep the ball rolling.*

- *"I thought someone else was taking care of that." Never assume. Excuses are roadblocks to action. Always ask questions to keep things moving.*

- *"No one told me" or "Nobody tells me anything." Let a manager or supervisor hear you talk this way and you will have made it clear that you operate in a tunnel, oblivious to everything around you, and take no responsibility.*

- *"I didn't have time." Don't bother with, "I was too busy," either. If you find yourself saying things like this, you are writing your own career obituary. If something matters, you make the time.*

- *"I didn't think I should ask about that." Remember the French menu? If you don't know, don't be afraid to say so. Only insecure people fear saying, "I don't know." Wise people ask, listen and learn. Above all:*

Remove disempowering statements form your vocabulary.

"If It's to Be, It's Up to Me."

I have a copy of this very sheet pinned on my office wall to the right of my computer screen. It's a constant reminder of what I can do to keep writing an empowering and true story about my life. I hope you'll do the same.

The message is clear and simple: effective, successful people don't make excuses. They create solutions. They **are** the solution. Whatever the roadblocks are, it's up to you to take responsibility and remove them. If not, you become one of them. To say it more simply with my favourite aphorism, "If it's to be, it's up to me!"

So step up and check your story. What do you tell others about yourself and why? More importantly, what account of the past are you reinforcing for your own mind? Is it an empowering one, where you accept your role in good and bad outcomes and become smarter and better as time passes? Or is it a horror story where you're the victim and everybody else is against you? Your answer will determine much about your future. You can't see your gap or think with a fresh perspective if you can't even acknowledge that things aren't right.

What do you tell others about yourself and why? More importantly, what account of the past are you reinforcing for your own mind?

Recently, I was enjoying lunch with a successful businesswoman called Jan.

Jan had been through the mill and was now living a happy, positive and successful life. We got onto the subject of self-realisation and empowerment and the liberating effect they have on one's life when you truly embrace them. Jan shared a little twist she adopted a few years back, when something goes wrong, Jan simply says with a smile and a laugh: 'Oh, well, it's my fault." It's not that Jan beats herself up – she just accepts the situation, assesses it and gets on with a solution. "Just get on with it!" she exclaimed. "I don't spend hours and days looking for someone to blame. That saves me a heap of time!"

Everything goes back to one fundamental principle: before you can sit in the Pilot's seat and take control of your destiny, you must take full responsibility for your choices, actions, consequences and relationships.

Everything goes back to one fundamental principle: before you can sit in the Pilot's seat and take control of your destiny, you must take full responsibility for your choices, actions, consequences and relationships. Swallow your pride, lose your blame mentality and look at your reflection. It's not as bad as you fear. In fact, accepting your mistakes and failings is liberating! It's a breath of fresh air for your spirit, and it will keep you going.

Key Questions

- What's the story I regularly tell other people?
- What's the story I tell myself about myself?
- Why do I tell that story?
- What aspects of my story are false and what do they hide?
- What's the worst that could happen if I looked at myself in the mirror and admitted to my role in my failures?

The Million-Dollar Question

How can I change my story from this point forward?

Knowledge Without Action is Worthless

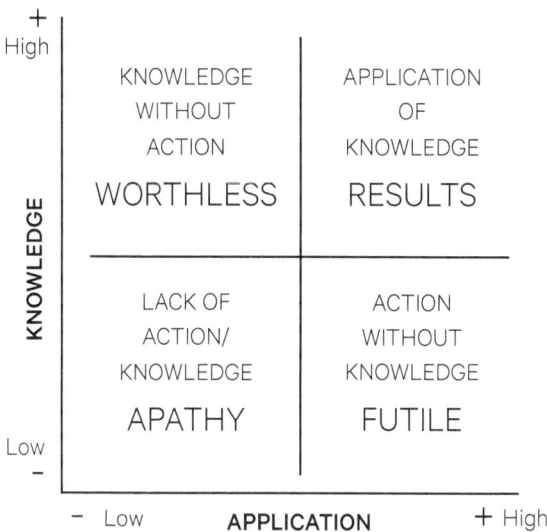

	APPLICATION Low (−)	**APPLICATION** High (+)
KNOWLEDGE High (+)	KNOWLEDGE WITHOUT ACTION **WORTHLESS**	APPLICATION OF KNOWLEDGE **RESULTS**
KNOWLEDGE Low (−)	LACK OF ACTION/ KNOWLEDGE **APATHY**	ACTION WITHOUT KNOWLEDGE **FUTILE**

"Knowledge isn't life changing. The application of knowledge is."

— Ted Stockor

"Knowing is not enough; we must apply. Willing is not enough; we must do."

—Johann Wolfgang von Goethe

As we approach the end of our "Pilot or Passenger" journey, I'd like you to ask yourself a question: with all the self-development books, gurus and seminars out there, why do so few people seem to be, you know, developing?

Eighty per cent of people who read this book or any other self-development book, or who go to seminars or hire personal coaches, will revert to their old ways.

You already know the answer, of course: the 80/20 Rule. Eighty per cent of people who read this book or any other self-development book, or who go to seminars or hire personal coaches, will revert to their old ways. They may want to be the Pilot and control their destiny, and they may know and understand that they must change in order to improve. But alas, it all gets too hard. It's much easier to fall back into the Matrix.

The worldwide self-development (also called self-improvement or self-help) culture takes in approximately $12 billion each year, most of it wasted. An entrepreneur by the name of Matthew Michalewicz cuts right to it in an article published in *Business Insider Australia*:

> ... *People aren't looking for the "secrets" to success, they're looking for the "shortcuts" to success. They want to get rich with no risk and no money down; they want to lose weight without diet or exercise; they want to look 20 years younger overnight, through creams, lotion and glitter.*
>
> *Effortless, simple, risk free! Those are the headlines that sell. No work required! And people buy and consume the hype, gorging themselves to the tune of $12 billion each year.*
>
> *They read the books, watch the DVDs and listen to the seminars. It makes them feel drunk, high. Their feet leave the ground and they spacewalk to the moon. Their dreams are*

alive and well, within reach, and it's effortless, simple, risk free – the books and seminars said so.

But weeks pass, then months, and of course, nothing changes in their life. Each evening they wish upon a Ferrari, and each morning they wake up disappointed.

Why? Because people mistake the gathering of knowledge for action. I refer to these people as "seminar junkies". They attend seminar after seminar, take in information, make lists and get fired up, ready to act. Then nothing. They always have a reason not to take the controls. There's always one last thing they need to do, one more seminar they need to attend or book they need to read. As soon as that's done, they'll be taking risks and changing things. But somehow, they never get out there. Ready, set, ready set, ready set ... but no fire! And of the 20 per cent who do, 80 per cent take off like rockets ... and, like rockets, they fall apart in stages.

They fail to understand Raw Fact #7:

Having information changes nothing.
Knowledge without action is worthless.

The propensity for millions of "self-help junkies" to get a drug-like high from self-help cheerleading, only to lose the high and crave it again, turns most self-development purveyors into little more than drug dealers servicing an addiction. I got a view of the abusive, ugly side of this subculture a few years ago when I met a young man I'll call George. He created a company that sold a range of marketing and business-development programs under license to aspiring entrepreneurs.

I went to a few of his seminars so see how he was winning so many acolytes, and he was really good. He had great charisma and knew how to work an audience, taking them through a journey of rapport, connection, desire and the pain of inaction. Then he would offer a solution: a golden pill, a silver bullet — his programs!

But as I spent more time with George and got to know him better, I saw how manipulative and unethical his operation was. For example, one of his offers was a "sub-license" — a license to use his brand and programs to create your own business. While the cost was about $10,000 initially, the addition of interest and fees pushed the total cost over five years to about $22,000. Making things even dodgier, he had a questionable "finance company" that gave high-risk loans at a very high and risky price.

One night, an 18-year-old girl – who was four months' pregnant, living at home with her parents and had a casual job at a supermarket – came to one of George's seminars and was totally taken in by the hype and excitement. At the end of the seminar, he sold her a "Business Consultant" sub-license on the spot for $10,000, financed. I couldn't believe what I was witnessing. I took the girl aside and suggested she go home, talk to her parents and think about it, but she was convinced that this was for her and she wanted the "sign up tonight" deal.

After the event, I spoke to George privately and said, "You can't do this. She's 18, she lives at home and she doesn't know anything about being a business consultant. She hasn't a hope in hell of being taken seriously; she'll never get a return on that license and you will have destroyed her financially." I could see this poor girl being in debt for the rest of her life because of this one mistake.

George had a predatory look in his eye and gave me his rationale. "Alex," he said, "how many times have you failed in business? We all have, haven't we? And every time we failed, it taught us something and spurred us on to bounce back harder and stronger than before, right? Yes, she's probably going to fail at this. I know that. It's going to cost her a lot of money, and it's going to take her and her family a long time to pay this money back. But failure changes people. This may be the *one* failure that changes her life for the better. So who am I to stand in the way of that failure?"

It was blatant, opportunistic manipulation of a vulnerable, inexperienced young woman. Fortunately, I had the contracts cancelled and the young lady learned a very valuable lesson from that encounter. This experience alone was enough to make me promise that I would never be a part of the traditional "sweet talk, sour results" self-development culture.

If the Want is Strong Enough, the How Will Happen

That's why this book pulls no punches. There's an old saying: "If it was easy, everybody would be doing it." Changing the course you're on is not easy; if it was, everyone would be in a career they loved and living the dream. Inertia is powerful. Once your life picks up speed on its current course, it takes a titanic effort to wrestle the controls from the auto-pilot system and steer your aircraft onto your new course. It takes consistent, unrelenting effort.

There are no short cuts. There are no magic prosperity pills. The law of attraction isn't a magic wand. It doesn't matter how hard you visualise and wish for something — it's not going to materialise out of thin air! If you want to change things, you have to take ownership, figure out where you're going, work out how to get there and take action over and over again. There's magic in disciplined repetition.

If you want to change things, you have to take ownership, figure out where you're going, work out how to get there and take action over and over again.

This book is about breaking the barrier between thought and action.

Part of what makes action effective is how you *prioritise* it — the order in which you do what you do. The order of things matters;

for example, it's hard to have a career as a nurse without going to nursing school first. That's why "reverse engineering" is such a powerful tool. By determining your desired outcomes, you can work back through the steps and stages you must navigate to reach your destination.

The great misconception is that all action is created equal. Just doing things isn't enough — being busy for the sake of being busy is counterproductive. You need to look at your flight path and determine what needs to be done first and what is likely to give you the best return on your investment of time, energy and effort. If you want to achieve, you need to ensure your actions are *meaningful.* What is meaningful action? It's action that contributes to your overall plan by moving you forward. Becoming mindful of meaningful actions will push you and keep you focused. It's part of the mindset that will keep you on course.

Meaningful Action

Sometime the actions we are required to take are radical and challenging. It's hard to get off the runway. We often need an "activating event" to spark us into action. What's going to be the activating event that propels you into meaningful action?

I have a friend who had to make a very difficult emotional decision: to sever his connections with family and lifelong friends and relocate to a different part of the country in order to escape their physiological and emotional hold. His only other choice was to remain in an environment surrounded by long term unemployed non-achievers and misery guts — people who were content to go through life on welfare as Passengers, bitching about the service in economy class. But he was different; he knew there was more to life than surviving on a weekly wage and complaining about all the "luck" that made others successful. But he knew that unless he took dramatic and meaningful action, nothing was ever going to change for him. So he did. It wasn't easy, but it changed his life for the better.

Relocating to another country to attend an elite technical college is meaningful action. Making a list of technical colleges is not. Planning, lists and posting on social networks — they can all be useful, but don't mistake them for action. Genuine meaningful action is risky yet exhilarating. It reflects the best parts of your personality: your passion, commitment and creativity. In fact, it *magnifies* those aspects of who you are. I've talked with people who told me that it was only by pushing aside their fears and launching their businesses or venturing into the unknown that they became who they truly thought they could be.

Genuine meaningful action is risky yet exhilarating. It reflects the best parts of your personality: your passion, commitment and creativity.

The trouble is, action can be frightening and disruptive to the status quo. It alienates people. It demands that you leap into the wilderness with only a compass and canteen. That's why so many people pacify their desire for change with the placebo of self-help bromides. They offer a feel-good quality without the fear of failure or embarrassment. But the fact that you have read this far, shows that's not what you want.

As Steve Simpson says: "When you are frustrated with your current state or have aspirations for something greater — do something."

So what is the want inside you that's strong enough to move mountains? What do you want that you can't live without? What's crawling around in your gut, trying to get out? Is there something you've thought about doing for years that if you don't try to make happen will haunt you for the rest of your life?

143

That's the power source for your leap into meaningful action. Your conscious mind is merely a receptor of the universe; its primary role is to gather information via your senses and pass it on to the subconscious, where the hard work takes place. The subconscious mind never sleeps. It's always working. It's the engine room of the self, always looking for solutions and opportunities. But you have to tell it what you want it to look for, and you need to be specific or it will discard your ideas as more "here we go again" dreaming.

The subconscious mind never sleeps. It's always working. It's the engine room of the self, always looking for solutions and opportunities.

Simply telling yourself that you want to make a lot of money, but not having a clear vision and plan for how much money you want, how you'll make it, when you'll make it and what you'll do with it, is like walking up to a bank teller, smiling and saying, "I'd like to withdraw some money, please." The teller would pause, stare at you and ask, "How much?" If you replied, "Oh I don't really know, just make it a lot," chances are that instead of getting money, you would get a visit from bank security.

This is where most books would have you do an action plan. I'm not going to do that just yet, because action plans are meaningless until you are eager and hungry for meaningful, exciting action. Until you use your subconscious to engage your emotions, you won't act. So forget about action plans and lists for now. Instead, I want you to seriously ponder and answer these questions:

1. *What do I really want my life to look like in five years?*

2. *What's the gap between where I am now and where I want to be — emotionally, psychologically, financially and in terms of skills and knowledge?*

———————————————————————

———————————————————————

3. *What choices have gotten me to where I am today, and what choices must I make to take me in the direction of what I want?*

———————————————————————

———————————————————————

Your Activating Event – Your Call to Action.

Convincing and motivating yourself into action is similar to selling. For you to "buy in", you first need to be aware of your situation and the change that's possible. From this awareness, you stoke your desire: to become a better you, to achieve your dream lifestyle and to reach your full intellectual, creative or economic potential. As this desire — this **need** — intensifies, it gets you thinking and looking for opportunities. Sounds simple, right? However, the facts speak for themselves — most people do not make the necessary changes to become the Pilots of their lives because they are comfortable. Not happy, but comfortably numb enough to tippy-toe through life safely to death.

I've talked briefly about the "activating event". It's when something happens in a person's life that gives them a wake-up call. It could be a divorce, the death of a loved one or close friend, or perhaps an illness. It might be a school reunion, the loss of a job or even a world event that resonates with you and makes you realise life is short.

For example, the September 11, 2001, attack on America was a massive wake-up call and activating event for millions of people around the world. The tragic and senseless loss of so many innocent lives stunned the world and brought home to many that life is fragile and precious. Post 9/11, many people took on a totally different view of their world and asked: "What do I really want out of life? What do I want to do, see and experience, and how badly do I want it?"

It was an activating event that snapped many people into action. They realised that being a Passenger moving unconsciously towards retirement and death was not for them. The event shook them into transforming their dreams into goals. It was a time when many Passengers earned their wings, became Pilots and never looked back.

The thing is, you don't need a disaster or a near-death experience to motivate you to act. The fact you have read this book alone shows that you have a desire to change things. All you need is a goal that you want so badly, you'll do anything to make it happen.

Goal Setting

As a Pilot, you would never dream of taking off on a journey without a flight plan, so why would you do it with your life? Knowing the route and waypoints and planning the stages and stopovers will not only ensure you arrive at your destination, but that you take off in the first place. Getting off the ground is the hardest part.

Remember, the only difference between a dream and a goal is a date. "A goal is a dream with a deadline" may be a cliché, but like many clichés, it's also true. Once you have the fire and desire to take meaningful action, you can't simply start running in every direction, hoping to trip over an opportunity. There are only so many hours in the day and so much money. Your actions should be as efficient as they are meaningful.

Remember, the only difference between a dream and a goal is a date. "A goal is a dream with a deadline" may be a cliché, but like many clichés, it's also true.

There's a terrific goal-setting format I came across many years ago called "SMART goals": Specific, Measurable, Attainable, Realistic and Tangible. This is what setting SMART goals means:

- **Specific**: This is the what, where, when and why. Your goals must clearly state what you want to achieve: the style of home you want, how much money you want to make, and so on.

- **Measurable**: Measurability applies to the destination and the path. How will you chart your progress – by dollars earned or miles travelled? Monitoring and measuring your milestones will keep you on course. Reverse engineer checkpoints into your journey.

- **Attainable**: People fail at their New Year's resolutions because they set goals that are unattainable. Somebody who's 50 kilos overweight and has never exercised is not going to lose 20 kilos by March! Make sure your goals are bold but reachable. Don't expect to change your world in 12 days or 12 weeks. Things are always twice as difficult as you think.

- **Realistic:** Your new smartphone design is not going to replace the iPhone and take down Apple. You might capture a niche market that could make you rich, though. One goal is delusional; the other is sensible. Know what's realistic for you *today*, keeping in mind that you can always set new, larger goals in the future.

147

- **Tangible**: Link your goals to physical outcomes. When you lose 35 kilos and run your marathon, you'll buy yourself a gorgeous new suit. When you reach $100,000 in savings for retirement, you'll treat yourself to a trip to the Maldives. When you start your business, you'll create a sweet mobile office on a sailboat, which you've always wanted to do. Tangible rewards are motivators and evidence of your progress.

No more excuses. Take the time to write some SMART goals. Make your goal list as detailed as possible. Start with the end in mind. Work backwards from the date you want to be over that gap between today and tomorrow. Reverse engineer everything from your goal. What timeframe is required to achieve each part of your goal? What resources are you likely to need, from money to good people? How will you keep yourself motivated and on course? How will you reward yourself when you reach milestones so you can persevere through rough weather?

That's the beginning. But because inertia is powerful, it's not always enough. You might need more.

Give Yourself No Choice – Don't Give Yourself an Out!

For me, the most powerful weapon in the self-development arsenal is **accountability**.

All's fair in love, war and changing your life, right? That's why you should be pulling out all the stops to ensure you don't stall and stop in your efforts to leave today's situation in favour of a better tomorrow. For me, the most powerful weapon in the self-development arsenal is *accountability*.

Human beings are experts at self-delusion. We make ourselves promises about the future, and then when the future becomes the

148

present we equivocate. We say, "Not yet. Next year." That's how you tiptoe through life safely to death. If you want the greatest possible chance of reaching your goals, you've got to make stopping your journey more painful than continuing.

Put yourself in a position where it's nearly impossible for you to stray from your new path. Put yourself under a bit of pressure. Remember, pain is a great motivator that will bring you pleasurable outcomes. Share your goals with your circle of influence so that quitting will embarrass you. Put something on the table that you can lose.

We make ourselves promises about the future, and then when the future becomes the present we equivocate. We say, "Not yet. Next year." That's how you tiptoe through life safely to death.

One example is to invest what I call "hurt money". For many years, I wanted to travel to the northern-most tip of Australia — Cape York. It's about 5,000km from where I live and the last leg of the trip is a testing, challenging 1,500km, four-wheel-drive-only trek through wilderness and scrub country. But it was a real adventure and a must-do on my bucket list. One day, I was at a travel show and there was a tour operator who ran "tag-along" tours to Cape York. He acted as a lead guide in his vehicle and paying clients would drive their own vehicles with him in convoy. The setup would provide safety and security, and I would not have to worry about being on my own, tackling the many crocodile-infested creek and river crossings. It was perfect! And, much to my surprise, I was free on the dates of the 12-day tour!

I was keen, it was on my must-do list, and the time and price were right – but I was still hesitant. I was looking for reasons *not* to commit: *What if a client needs me? What if a get a booking?*

Finally, my wife said, "Come on, Alex, you know you want to do this. It's the best opportunity you'll get. Put some hurt money down!" She was right. I smiled, pulled out the credit card and paid a 50 per cent non-refundable deposit. I was, in poker terms, "all in".

During the months prior to the holiday, I had several requests for bookings during the dates of the trip. I know in my heart that had I not put the deposit down, I would have locked in those speaking dates and not gone to Cape York. Chances are, years later I still wouldn't have made it to "the tip". But I did go, and it was one of the best holidays of my life!

The other personal example of giving myself no choice is this book. I told many of my friends and associates I was writing a book, so that every time I spoke to them, often the first thing that came out of their mouths was: "How's the book going?" Some days, I just didn't want to write, but as I mentioned earlier, we hate looking stupid. To keep from humiliating myself, I simply had to finish the book. So I did.

Set goals and commit to action that leaves little or no room for getting lazy and dropping your bundle. This will, at first, seem terrifying, but it will become liberating!

Accountability also comes when you cut ties and make change irreversible. You can't go back because there's nothing to go back to.

Accountability also comes when you cut ties and make change irreversible. You can't go back because there's nothing to go back to. That's especially true when people think about leaving a job they no longer enjoy. There are always reasons to stay, and the biggest is the fear of the unknown. We prefer known misery to the unknown potential for joy! It's twisted. So I ask people: "If they fired you tomorrow, what would you do?" The answer is normally, "I'd take a long holiday," or, "I'd find a new and better job," or, "I'd start my own business." So why not fire yourself and take control of the process? Make it happen now, because if you're miserable and not performing, one day the decision will be made for you.

The same is true if you're in an unhappy relationship with someone who doesn't support you, if you're tried to fix it and it's just not working, fire your spouse or partner! Why would you stay with someone who's an anchor on your aspirations? The end can be slow and painful, dragging you through depression and acrimony at a time when you need all your energy to build your new life. Or it can be conscious, quick and empowering. And if you don't do it, odds are your partner eventually will.

So why not fire yourself and take control of the process? Make it happen now, because if you're miserable and not performing, one day the decision will be made for you.

This action may seem rash and impetuous, but you've probably known you needed to make the move for a long time; you just haven't done it. This is a stark example of the difference between being the Pilot or Passenger in your life. This is the time to choose — to take control!

Accountability also comes when you give others permission to hold you accountable. Be accountable to someone, perhaps a mentor, coach or close friend. Create a system that doesn't let you off the hook. Why do people hire personal trainers to help them become fit? It's not because they don't know how to do push-ups; any eight year old knows how to do them. It's because they need someone to show up at their home at six o'clock in the morning and make them *do* the push-ups!

We all have blind spots. We're all a little self-delusional. We all procrastinate. That's why I encourage people to find "accountability partners" – friends who will hold you to your promises and goals. When I present seminars and workshops on goal setting, I buddy people up to hold each other accountable. I ask each participant to write a cheque for $1,000 (or provide a credit card number) to their favourite charity and to give it to their "buddy". If at the end of 12 weeks they have not achieved their SMART goals, their buddy has permission to post their cheque (or process their credit card) and give the money to the chosen charity.

It's amazing what putting down a bit of "hurt money" can achieve. Almost everyone achieved their goals, not because they didn't want to donate the $1,000 but because they didn't want to appear to be failures. We have the power to help each other be better. Change is difficult enough; you don't have to do it alone. Buddy up.

GOALS WORKSHEET

My main goal:

_____

My deadline:

_____

The incremental goals I must achieve along the way:

_____

_____

What makes my goal:

SPECIFIC: _____

MEASURABLE:_____

ATTAINABLE: _____

REALISTIC: _____

TANGIBLE: _____

The return I want from my investment in my goal is:

TIME RETURN: _____

LIFESTYLE RETURN: _____

I Will Know I Have Reached My Goal When The Following Happens:

_____

_____

_____

Get in Goal Condition

So, are you going to be a Pilot or a Passenger? Visualise your life as a journey by air. You may have to divert because of bad weather, but as long as you have your destination locked in, you're fine. You may have to land to let a storm pass, but then you can refuel and get back on course. The key question isn't whether you'll fly, but whether you'll be the Pilot or the Passenger.

Eighty per cent of the people in this world are Passengers. They're perfectly content to let someone else be in control of their journey, because either they don't feel worthy of taking the controls or they're too frightened or lazy.

Eighty per cent of the people in this world are Passengers. They're perfectly content to let someone else be in control of their journey, because either they don't feel worthy of taking the controls or they're too frightened or lazy. They're the ones who follow culture blindly, regret what they don't do, and tiptoe right into their graves.

We have all been conditioned to veer towards the easy path, but you can re-condition your mind to focus on your potential. I've told you about the importance of engaging your emotions and going after what you really, truly want. That starts now.

Whatever it is you want to achieve – taste it, desire it and take the action you need to get it. Do one thing. Do it successfully. Then do another, then another. A journey of a thousand miles begins with a single step. As you achieve your goals, they will make a positive difference in your life. You'll gain motivation. You'll reshape how you see yourself. You'll become a different person, someone who asks, "Why not?" instead of "Why?"

154

Don't give yourself a chance to back out! Be honest about how your brain works and understand how to work around your conditioning and natural human fear of change. Your life is not a life sentence. It's yours to celebrate and enjoy.

One last piece of advice: put this book down. Don't buy another one. Figure out what you hunger for, make a commitment, set goals and take action.

You can change from this day forward.

Will you?

Remember, "If it's to be, it's up to me."

Step into the cockpit. Take the controls. Burst through the clouds and seize the day ... Captain!

Key Questions

- Have I embraced the placebo of self-help culture before? What's it gotten me?
- When was the last time I took meaningful action towards what I want?
- What kind of different choices do I need to make to get the outcomes I want?
- In retrospect, have there been activating events in the past I've ignored or misinterpreted? What were they and what were they trying to tell me?
- What's my big life goal? How Specific, Measurable, Attainable, Realistic and Tangible is it?
- What smaller goals must I reach to make my big goal possible?
- What can I do to give myself no choice but to keep moving despite my fear and doubt?

- Who can be my accountability partners?
- What do I want my world to look like in 5 years' time? What will it look like if nothing changes?

The Million-Dollar Question

What DO I want more than anything? What's the thing I simply can't NOT do?

Tools & Tips

Don't over complicate things. Doing this is simple. You can buy another book, watch another DVD or attend another seminar – or you can take action and make things happen.

Grab a pen. Fast-forward five years in your mind and visualise your world. Write that letter to your friend, and turn it into your flight plan by reverse engineering it. Then make it happen. Remember, if the want is strong enough, the how will happen.

- **Tools**: Don't over complicate them – all you need is a pen, paper and clear mind!
- **Tips**: Just do it NOW. Plan the flight and Fly the plan. Keep your eye on the prize and visualise how great it's going to be when you get there.

I have genuinely written this book with the best intentions to help you learn from my successes, failures, strengths and weaknesses. I want to give you a few gems I wish I had been given earlier in my journey. If any of this book has resonated with you, has stopped you to think and reflect and has ignited a desire within you to act, then my life is all the richer.

Underpin your journey with the values of honesty, respect and commitment. Be mindful of the moment and enjoy your journey – wherever you decide to fly.

Finally, if you would like to share your "wins", email me at alex@
alexbonett.com. I would love to hear from you.

You are cleared for takeoff!

*Helping Individuals, Teams and Businesses
Engage at the Highest Possible Level.*

From 'Trolley Boy' to leading Multi Million Dollar Companies, Alex draws from a wealth of 40 years of Real, Practical, 'Warts & All', Hands on Experience!

His passionate, quick thinking and witty approach to training Individuals, Teams and Businesses to Achieve Real and Lasting Results will have you both laughing and crying in your seats. But above all, the end result will be a total mind shift to a Brighter, Happier & More Productive Future

With 40 years of experience in the retail and service sectors. Alex has worked in key positions within some of Australia's most successful private and public companies.

As GM of revenue centre's as large as a quarter of a billion dollars, Alex understands the building blocks of long-term growth and profitability in business. In the past 12 years, Alex has presented to thousands of Business Owners and Managers around the country and their Employees helping them understand 'The Psychology Behind Success' and the art of Sales, Service and Performance by 'Playing at the Pointy End"

Alex is also a co-author of the highly acclaimed "Two Worlds Unite" program, written specifically for the Australian Complementary Medical industry.

Putting into practice what Alex passionately believes in, he also created one of Australia's Leading Jewellery Wholesale Companies, from zero to a multimillion-dollar company in just a few years.

Today, Alex specialises in delivering highly inspirational and motivational presentations, improving personal and organisational performance by 'Helping Individuals, Teams and Businesses Engage at the Highest Possible Level'.

Conference Keynotes, Post conference; Training, Coaching, Co Mentoring (Groups), Masterclasses & Workshops and Consulting.

So let me know if you think
You, your Business or your Workplace would benefit from some Personal/Customised 'Pilot Training'.

Learn more at
www.alexbonett.com
Or drop me a note on alex@alexbonet.com

Staying in the Circle...and Maintaining the Mindset

Thank you for investing your time into this book.

I truly hope it has reignited a renewed passion for breaking out of the ordinary, getting out of the passenger seat and taking control of your destiny.

I speak and consult on this very subject as well as my other passions

Sales, Service and Performance – '*Playing at the Pointy End'*

" Helping Individuals, Teams & Businesses Engage at the Highest Possible Level" by inspiring people to Engage.

Here is what others had to say...

Wow. Alex is one of the most enthusiastic, powerful and results-oriented speakers I have every experienced.

– Andrew Wies, National Marketing Manager

Fantastic, straight to the point. Excellent 'new' ideas not already around. Alex's enthusiasm and passion for marketing is overwhelming... 'Show me the money!'

– Catherine Powell, Business Owner

www.ingramcontent.com/pod-product-compliance
Lightning Source LLC
LaVergne TN
LVHW021451080426
835509LV00018B/2243